THE RUSTIC GARDEN

THE
RUSTIC
GARDEN

Jean Stone

B.T. Batsford Ltd · London

for Victoria Emma, Charlotte Hannah and Francesca Sophia

First published 1992

Typeset by Lasertext Ltd., Stretford, Manchester

and printed in Great Britain by Mackays of Chatham Ltd.

Published by
B.T. Batsford Ltd
4 Fitzhardinge Street
London W1H 0AH

A catalogue record for this book is available from
the British Library

ISBN 0 7134 6548 4

CONTENTS

LIST OF ILLUSTRATIONS

Black and white

ACKNOWLEDGEMENTS

I first began researching rustic garden architecture and furniture as part of a course on 'The Conservation of Historic Landscape Parks and Gardens' at the Architectural Association, London. I would, therefore, like to extend thanks to my tutors, Edward Fawcett and Gordon Ballard, and to other course participants who have given their help and encouragement, particularly Joyce Bellamy, Judy Conway, Jane Crawley, Annette Lace, Christopher Sumner, and Marion Woodward.

Course completed, I next entered the *Sunday Times* 'Design a Period Garden' competition and, as winner, my 'Victorian Rustic Garden' was built at the Royal Horticultural Society Chelsea Flower Show, 1989, where it won a Silver Flora Medal. My thanks go to Toni Clarke, who did the accompanying illustrations for the entry; Jill Wrightson, for the planting scheme; the Endersby brothers, who built the individual rustic features for the garden; and L. John Bailey for his patience and expert craftsmanship, and his care in giving the garden all those final little touches.

I am indebted to many other people who have helped more directly with the preparation of this book: Mrs Margaret Richards, for steering me through the archives at Badminton, and Tim Knox for similar guidance at the British Architectural Library; Peter Day, Keeper of the Chatsworth Collections; Graham Dalling of Enfield Libraries; Ms D. Rawlinson of the Jenner Museum; Brent Elliott of the Lindley Library; Charles Hind and Jackie Rees of Sotheby's; Mr R. J. Berkeley of Spetchley Park; Patrick Goode; Christopher Dingwall; Nigel Temple; the staff at the British Library and the National Trust; J. Buckland, Head Gardener at West Dean; Martin Heymann, Agent at West Dean; David Wadsworth and The Hon. Mrs Jane Roberts, Curator of The Print Room, The Royal Library, Windsor Castle.

I would particularly like to thank my friends for their continued help and enthusiasm: Vera Dawkins, Barbara Simpson Lee, Erik de Graaff, Carol Antinou, Christoph Egret, Marian Griffiths, John and Heather Harvey, Matthew Marchbank, Rose Michel, and Keith and Clare Taylor.

Thank you to my family: my mother, my daughter Sarah, and daughter-in-law Joanne, for their interest; my cousin Ann Thomas, for her companionship on some very long drives; and in particular, my son Max for endless patience and telephone tuition on how to use the word processor!

INTRODUCTION

The rustic garden is one that depends on the use of unhewn branches, twigs, and even roots for the construction of its architecture, furniture and ornament. There are a few exceptions to these criteria, such as picturesque and quaint huts and cottages from distant climes; these, because we associate them with more primitive cultures and their construction or decorations, hold a particular appeal that satisfies the romantic instinct; we are thus happy to include them in the rustic setting.

The word 'rustic'; brings to mind a picture of rural charm: the village green, its water pump and pond, waddling ducks, grazing sheep and cattle, low thatched roofs of barns and cottages, and rustic porches with roses round the doors. It is no wonder that the charm of rusticity should have lingered on to provide a sham rural setting in the garden where one can escape to a poetic land of fantasy. Such a garden is a humble land, where man can feel at one with nature, a land where innate creative instincts are nurtured.

After nourishment, man's second need is shelter and warmth, and these comforts were provided for archaic man by the tree and the cave. They gave shelter from bad weather, shade from the sun and protection from foes and wild beasts. It is perhaps for this reason that the image of the tree has continued to be honoured as a sacred image of life and fertility. This image has travelled down the ages since ancient mythology; from the story of the Garden of Eden to the philosophy of the Romantic Movement, when William Blake (1757–1827) and his contemporaries concerned themselves with the relationship between man's spiritual life and the vegetal life surrounding him. It was, indeed, the literature and paintings of the Romantic Movement that came to provide the backdrop for 'the rustic taste' (as it came to be known). No longer did rigid architectural orders take precedence in the garden. The way was now open for a return to the primitive and to the natural; and rusticity was the choice that satisfied the Romantic spirit, bringing a closeness to nature and offering an escape to an unknown world of the imagination.

Woodland industries have always been a vital part of country life, and rustic architecture and furniture-making grew out of the many traditional woodland crafts practised since earliest times by the rural labourer. Our present awareness of the advantages of conservation and the disastrous effect of pollution, and our attitude to the preservation of trees show that nature is respected once again. The countryside is often littered with surplus timber after winds and storms, providing the ideal opportunity for modern man to try his hand at creating a rustic garden. Fallen timber offers as much scope as (if not more than) finished wood, is far less expensive, and does not necessitate the felling of trees to supply working materials.

The wild garden is now enjoying a vogue, and what more appropriate in such a setting than a rustic seat, or a summerhouse? The most unskilled carpenter can 'have a go' at making rustic features; only a very few basic carpentry skills are necessary, and if your first attempts are not presentable to the outside world, then cover them with creeper! A primitive finish should not be despised, it can lend an attractive crudeness, an unsophisticated, even clownish quality to a garden feature, which can then become part of that world of grotesque rusticity associated with muses and magic and the haunts of hermits.

It needs just a little creative ingenuity to come up with a new rustic design. Rustic features often rely on the kind and shapes of timber available to the craftsman, which can range from the long straight poles of larch available from garden centres, to the gnarled and knotty pieces from storm-damaged trees, but it is the creative ingenuity of the individual's imagination that plays the most important part in producing a unique design. Creativity is inborn in all of us and in creating a rustic garden you will also be creating a little world of caprice and fantasy away from the turmoil of modern life.

1
CASTLE AND FARM

Medieval gardens were not rustic in the way that we think of rustic gardens today, built with rough-hewn logs and misshapen branches, but they contained many features, built of wood, which would be in harmony with the modern rustic garden. No original gardens of the Middle Ages remain, but we do know, from illuminated manuscripts, paintings, woodcut prints and early literature, how they might have looked. The farm garden would have been a garden of utility, where vegetables and herbs were cultivated for consumption, rather than grown for their beauty. Castle gardens, and gardens of noblemen, on the other hand, would have been gardens for pleasure and outdoor entertainment.

Timber was used quite extensively in these early days, and in the castle garden one would have found roofs of shingles or thatch, as well as rustic arbours and tunnels, grown over with shade-giving plants. Trellis work and fences were made from split coppiced poles, or, where privacy and protection from the weather was a priority, woven wattle hurdles were erected. Features around the farm and in the farm garden were built using the same methods of construction and from similar materials, but they were built for practical purposes rather than garden ornament.

It was in the shade of the tunnel arbour, or leafy bower, that medieval ladies might have strolled or sat, protecting their prized pale complexions from the summer sun. Early arbours were formed with poles of juniper or willow, and bound together with osiers. Young timber is the most satisfactory material for this purpose, particularly chestnut poles or larch, which are supple and springy and will therefore arch easily. Traditionally the poles were tied together with willow cords or briar, but a modern alternative, which lasts longer, is galvanized wire, which can be disguised by burnishing it to a dark colour and knotting in the traditional way.

Early trellis work too, was often made by knotting coppiced poles or laths together. Nowadays, as well as light trellis, many garden centres stock a heavier criss-cross trellis made from round chestnut, split in two and stripped of its bark, which is very suitable for fencing. Arches are also sold ready-made and both these and trellis work are ideal for the simple, rustic garden. Needless to say, today they are constructed with hammer and nails, rather than knotted willow cords!

To give more support to a tunnel arbour and to create a basic framework that will both outlast the timber, and make it easier to replace when the time comes, it is a good idea to include some iron arches in your construction. If these are painted brown, they will soon blend in with the planting, and if some coppiced poles remain visible the arbour will retain the appearance of a traditional timber arbour.

The choice of climbers for covering an arbour is extensive. It is generally believed

An octagonal summerhouse, or basket-house, so called because its sides are made of basket-weave panels set into a larch frame

that the rose has always been popular, and indeed, it can give spectacular results. However, one may be surprised to learn, from the writings of Didymus Mountaine in 1577, that, since rose arbours require a great deal of attention, vines were more frequently used to clothe arbours in medieval England.[1] This was also because the wild brier rose and the musk rose were the only true climbers available in England at that time. Cucumbers and gourds were alternatives to roses in the early seventeenth century, and as well as being decorative, they also offered useful crops.

In Queen Eleanor's Garden, Winchester, there is a tunnel arbour in which the plants have been chosen to create a continuous display. They include roses and, for early interest, a drapery of honeysuckle, or woodbine, *Lonicera periclymenum* 'Belgica', whose yellow flowers tinged with purple-red make a fine show before the vines 'Madeline Angevine' (a white grape) and 'Wrotham Pinot' (a black grape) start to display their fruits. By September, the woodbine bears its red berries, which glow in bright contrast to the rich black and succulent green grapes (Plate 1).

A pentice (a lean-to structure) is at the far end of Queen Eleanor's garden. A replica of what might have been found in a medieval castle garden, this was used as a sheltered walkway between one building and another. The roof is clad with cleft oak shingles. Now weathered to a silver colour, they glint in the sunshine, making a perfect foil to the white doves who have made their home in a corner under the eaves, and perch there to enjoy the comfort of the timbers warmed by the sun.

Shingles are pieces of sliced wood, which are used in the same way as tiles, or slates: to dress roofs, and sometimes walls. They have been used world-wide, throughout history, particularly in densely forested areas such as northern Europe, Australia, Canada, the USA, Russia, and Kashmir.

The kind of timber used for shingles varies from country to country, depending on what is grown locally, or is easily imported. Popular woods include fir, larch, sweet chestnut, and North American red cedar. In England, the traditional wood for handmade shingles was oak, the straighter the better in order that it might be cleft, and cut into pieces either four inches broad and eight inches long, or the larger size, eight inches broad and twelve inches long. Today, however, machine-cut cedar shingles are widely available, they are cheaper than oak, and easier to handle. The slices of wood are thicker at one end and can be easily cut into one of the many traditional shapes, either pointed or rounded, to give a fish-scale effect. Some of the finest examples of wooden architecture are to be found in Russia, where one will see shingles, centuries old, cut into a step pattern.

In most parts of the world today, the use of shingles on residential buildings is

Knotted laths were used for trellis work

Shingles make a pleasant alternative to thatch in the rustic garden

discouraged as they are considered a fire hazard. Nevertheless, shingles are aesthetically pleasing and, used on garden buildings as an alternative to thatch, they give lasting pleasure.

'The Sprout House', designed by Richard and Janet Strombeck, is a very unusual, modern all-purpose garden building which uses shingles to their full advantage. A pretty addition for the modern rustic garden, it is simply constructed, and useful as a potting-shed, a storage space, or even a playroom, as well as an ideal place to get your seedlings started in the spring, and to protect plants from winter weather.

Herbs have been cultivated since early times, and provide a pretty feature in a rustic garden. In the Middle Ages herbs played a vital role in everyday life, and were grown for a variety of purposes: for cooking; as remedies for illness (both physical and mental); for cosmetic uses; for making dyes for wool and cloth; and frequently as an ingredient of the paint used for illuminating manuscripts. Although for a number of years only a few favourites continued to be grown in our gardens, herb gardens are once again very popular. We now know that many old wives' tales about the use of herbs are not so ridiculous as we once thought, and herbs are often used in what is now called 'alternative' medicine. Oriental cookery may have also re-introduced many old herbs to western countries.

Now that the use of insecticides is discouraged, it is worth remembering that aromatic herbs grown in the garden will discourage insect attack on neighbouring plants. What looks more attractive than a multitude of herbs growing along the base of a rose trellis, or around the standards in the rose garden, with the additional satisfaction of knowing that aphids will be kept at bay?

There is limited documentary evidence about the gardens of medieval cottages and farmhouses, but a farm garden has recently been re-created around 'Bayleaf', an early sixteenth-century farmhouse in the Weald and Downland Open Air Museum, Singleton, West Sussex. At that time it was customary to grow herbs near the house, in beds raised slightly above the ground, and retained by a plank on edge. The beds were long and narrow in design so that the herbs could be tended without having to step on the beds. Traditionally, a decorative way of edging the beds would have been to board them with split logs, or with a narrow edging of wattle.

At Bayleaf, in keeping with the medieval style, there is a row of narrow herb beds in front of the farmhouse, each enclosed with a low edging of hazel wattle of about one foot high, using locally coppiced hazel. This is a traditional edging, not seen today, but one that could be used as a decorative way to contain herb beds in a rustic garden. A variety of herbs are grown in the beds at Bayleaf, and for the prominent central bed, some herbs that are not commonly grown today have been chosen. The common hyssop, *Hyssopus officinalis*, which has spikes of purple flowers is grown, along with 'Roseus' (pink) and 'Albus' (white). These three have been interspersed with winter savory, *Satureia montana*. Today, both hyssop and savory are rather neglected

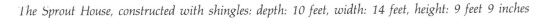

The Sprout House, constructed with shingles: depth: 10 feet, width: 14 feet, height: 9 feet 9 inches

Savory and hyssop grow in this herb bed with a woven-hazel border

plants, but in early times hyssop had pride of place in every country garden. Not only was it useful for cooking, but it was also thought to be something of a 'cure-all', and used particularly for chest complaints. Hyssop can be clipped back to form a low hedge and bears a profusion of flowering stems from July until early autumn. Winter savory is a hardy, quite shrubby, almost evergreen plant that makes a decorative companion to the hyssop; it grows about 12 inches high and bears pretty lilac-blue flowers. In earlier times it was grown mainly for its peppery flavour; and used as an alternative to pepper, which became so expensive that it almost priced itself off the market.

A herb garden, brim-full with plants, appeals to all the senses. It is pretty to look at, pleasant to smell, stimulating to touch, and the hum of the bees on their journey from flower to flower will soothe even the most restless of souls.

Beyond the herb beds at Bayleaf, are plots of the vegetables and salads that would have been grown in medieval times: brassicas, cabbages and turnips, leeks and onions, lettuce, and spinach beet. The complete garden, including the orchard of apples and pears, is enclosed by a fence comprising woven wands of coppiced hazel; an attractive and simple device for giving the crops protection from wind and weather.

Wattled-hazel hurdles, or close-braided osier hurdles, are indispensable in the windswept garden. They can also be used by the gardener to establish a hedge around the estate or garden, and, after the hedge has grown, the hurdles can be left in position to give added protection. The ordinary hazel hurdle gives a fence six-foot high, but lower fencing is sometimes available. The fence can be secured to posts and wire, and a four-inch board nailed along the top of a high fence will give it a firm finish. The colour of new, split hazel can be toned down with wood preservative.

Turf seats are frequently seen in old manuscripts and can be copied very easily. Start by building a low brick or stone wall about 18 inches high, parallel to, and about 18 inches from a higher garden wall, which will form the back of the seat. Build up the ends to 18 inches to form an open, box-shaped framework. Leave small gaps between one or two of the bricks at ground level, to allow excess water to seep out. Packed with earth, on a base of gravel for drainage, this box-shaped structure will be very firm, and the top of the seat can be upholstered with turf and low-growing wild flowers. Alternatives are chamomile, or perhaps creeping thyme. For a prettier, and more rustic effect, the brickwork, and the part of the garden wall forming the back of the seat can be faced with wattle panels cut from a wattle hurdle.

A woven fence is a useful support for climbing plants. Shoots of roses, clematis, and ivy can weave their way in and out of the verticals if the lower half is closely braided and top half left open. Many early manuscripts and illustrations depict wattle being used as garden fencing, and, as well as forming an admirable windbreak, it is also a pretty method of dividing off a part of a garden that one wishes to remain private. Unsightly views, or features such as compost heaps or dustbins, can be prettily concealed by a hurdle fence, too (Plate 2).

Rustic hurdles of woven willow or hazel have been used over many centuries for practical purposes, such as the protection of cattle, and the building of cottages and barns. Even the huts of the early Britons were made of wattle, which was sometimes daubed, thatched with straw or reed, and then lined with animal skins. It was not unusual for farm outbuildings to be left undaubed, and the illustration here shows a timber-framed building once used to house a tread-wheel. It has an infill of woven-hazel panels between the timbers and is covered by a roof of thatch. Obviously strong, long-lasting, and very attractive, this design would be very suitable for a garden, if cut down to summerhouse size.

An idea followed up by Sir James Hall MP, a Scottish country gentleman, might also be found inspiring. At the end of the eighteenth century Neo-Gothic architecture was very popular, and fast becoming accepted as the correct mode for churches far and wide. Sir James, eminent geologist and chemist, developed a theory that the essential parts of Gothic architecture derived from simple wattle buildings, reproduced in stone. When travelling and seeing peasants use long rods or poles as supports for vines, it occurred to him that ancient rustic dwellings might have been constructed of such rods, 'bearing a resemblance to works of Gothic architecture, and from which the peculiar forms of that style might have been derived.'[2] Hall put his ideas first into an essay and later, in 1813, published *The Origin and Principles of Gothic Architecture*. He also decided to test his theory and, with the help of 'an ingenious country workman, John White, a cooper in the village of Cockburnspath, Berwickshire',[3] at the beginning of spring, 1792, he began to construct a miniature 'willow cathedral', which was completed the following winter. He went about this by collecting a set of ash posts, about three inches in diameter, and setting them into the ground in two rows, at four-foot intervals. Then a number of slender and tapering willow rods, ten foot in length, were bound to the posts at their tops and pulled together to form a frame for a thatched roof. The finished building exhibited all the features of the Gothic style and far exceeded Hall's expectations in this respect. Although miniature, it was very substantial, and one could enter it quite comfortably. A drawing was made by

The tread-wheel house has panels of woven hazel

the young Alexander Carse, from Edinburgh,[4] and his view of the *Willow Cathedral*, painted with watercolour and a hint of gouache, was said to be a very accurate description (Plate 3).

A somewhat eccentric idea, this quaint yet pretty structure is an excellent example of what could be achieved in woven willow for a garden building; many designs could be derived from the same principles, although it would be easier to use pre-formed panels. The woven doors and windows would make very attractive gates when used in conjunction with a wattle fence, and would be a useful way of breaking up a dense run of fence. However, if you decide to construct a summerhouse in this way, take heed and learn from Sir James Hall, who had a slight problem the following year when 'a great number of rods struck root and throve well'![5] (Plate 4)

The Somerset Levels are an area of outstanding natural beauty and the environment is particularly suitable for willows, which grow there naturally and, consequently, have been cultivated as a crop for centuries. The first evidence of their use is a collection of wicker fragments unearthed from the Glastonbury Lake village of 100 BC, and the tradition of growing willows, weaving willow baskets, and making willow hurdles continues today.

Simplicity is an important factor in a rustic garden and its furniture, and features made from woven rustic hurdles have the appearance of being very simply made. However, much time and energy goes into growing and coppicing hazel for hurdle making, and in the process of growing, cutting, and weaving willow hurdles. There are secrets of manufacture too, handed down from generation to generation. In the past, the timber used for hurdle making in England varied around the country, according to what was grown locally – hazel or willow. However, it is said that willow hurdles are to be favoured for the garden, since they stand up to dampness more succesfully than hazel. Their appearance too, is neater than hazel.

Traditionally, wattle fencing was often woven *in situ* where it was needed, but now ready-made panels can be provided for fences, as well as components for wattle features, to be put together by the handyman in his own garden. The DIY man could easily and cheaply construct a simple summerhouse from hurdles. Even thatching the roof of a summerhouse with a roof of wattle is quite straightforward; hurdles can be thatched with heather in an amateur way without difficulty, and this gives good insulation as well as looking very pretty, even if it does not last so long as a professional job.

Heather, which is very durable, must be laid on in overlapping rows, with the bloom pointing downwards, and tied down with tarred string. The last two rows are laid the other way round, to hide the stalks and to give a neat finish.

There is a very valuable, old-fashioned country method of protecting plants with thatched hurdles: simply lay the thatched hurdles over frames, or support them by stakes, resting at an angle, over the growing crops. This will give the plants protection from frost, cold winds, and snow in winter, all for very little expense.

Thatching is, of course, expensive, but a little-known alternative is 'pine thatching'. This quaint substitute has been used very successfully in regions where quantities of pine needles can be gathered, and it is a very simple operation to carry out. First, the building must be roofed with boards covered with waterproof roofing felt, or roofing paper. Next, a heavy coating of tar or pitch is applied (this is most easily carried out with a broad, flat brush). Finally, pine needles are generously sprinkled on to the fresh pitch or tar, as thickly as they can be made to hold them. This gives the appearance of thatching, and is said to be quite durable if the boarded roof surface is well coated with tar or pitch.

For those less inclined to DIY, The English Basket Centre has been very enterprising, and is now marketing a wide range of woven-willow garden features, including seats, screens, arches, gates, bowers, bridges, and plant climbers, as well as custom-made articles. Features constructed from woven-willow panels are enjoying a revival, and often appear at such events as the Chelsea Flower Show, and other 'garden festivals', where they create enormous interest.

A garden built upon a theme of Somerset woven-willow features from The English Basket Centre was designed by Alan Sargent, for The Chelsea Flower Show in 1989, as a peaceful garden for town and country. It contains a summerhouse built with woven Somerset willow, and this theme is continued by willow-hurdle fencing, a post

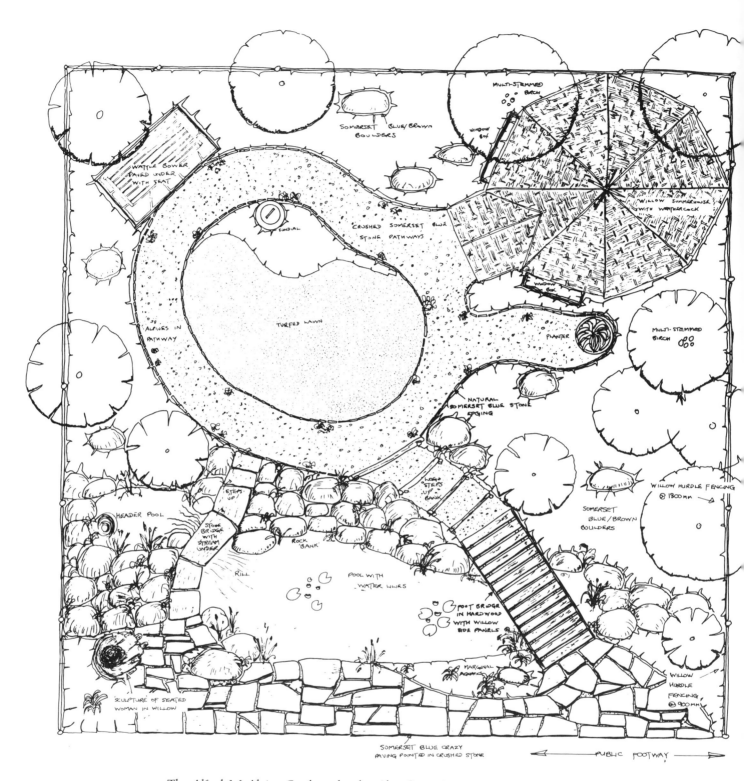

The Alfred McAlpine Garden, plan by Alan Sargent

bridge with woven-willow side panels, and log steps leading to a lawn and woven bower from which the whole garden can be admired. It is a true Somerset garden; even the paths and pavement are of natural blue Somerset stone. The path gravel and edgings are of crushed blue stone, whilst Somerset blue-brown boulders are reflected in the warm brown of the willow features (Plate 5).

Woven willow harmonizes beautifully with rustic features constructed with natural logs, and, for this reason, I used wattle to line the bank of the stream in my Victorian Rustic Garden at the 1989 Chelsea Flower Show. Wattle was once used for lining the banks of country streams to keep them tidy, especially if the banks were in danger of collapsing, and this idea can be transferred very successfully to a less formal country garden. Woven willow has a life of about six years when used in this way to decorate an ornamental water feature and, arranged carefully, it is a very attractive method of decorating a pool or stream. If the water feature is natural, or formed from puddled clay, a panel can be easily fixed to the bank with pegs made from willow. However, if the water feature is lined with a plastic liner it is important to peg the wattle carefully through the plastic liner above the water line, so as not to damage the lining and thus allow water to seep through. Alternatively, the top of the wattle can be kept in place with wire (the green plastic-covered variety), tied onto pegs and secured below the surface of the turf or stone edging the stream or pond (Plate 6).

To line the banks of a stream with woven willow, first line the trench with a plastic liner, but take care not to puncture this when putting the willow in place

For visual effect it is a good idea to line only part of the feature in this way. For instance, if it is a stream, line one bank with wattle, and edge the bank on the other side with contrasting silver birch or elm logs. If the feature takes the form of a pool, wattle could be used on one side and, on a shallow bank, very large, smooth stones would balance the design. However, if there are no banks, a stream running through large pebbles will look very effective in a rustic garden. If the pool of water is large enough to have ducks, nesting baskets, once found in England and still sometimes seen in France, make a practical yet attractive ornamental feature (Plate 7). When used in a formal pond with concrete sides these baskets add a bit of rustic cosiness, but on a pond with banks lined with wattle they echo this feature, and blend in perfectly to make a still more attractive scene. Rustic duck shelters in the centre, or by the side of a pond are an unusual feature these days, but much appreciated by ducks and swans in hot sunny weather (Plate 8).

A wattle garden is also a good idea for a roof garden, where weight and protection from the wind is of the utmost importance. A wattle fence can be erected, cemeted over, and made to look like a strong wall, even though it can be demolished very easily when the time comes. Woven furniture is light, and therefore very suitable for roof gardens. In the 1920s, when the Modern Movement gave a new importance to the roof garden, lightweight woven-willow furniture was very popular, and amongst the many features available were tables with woven-willow sunshades. Unfortunately, these are not generally available today, but what a lovely idea!

2

THE NATURAL STYLE

In the early eighteenth century England found herself emerging from a period of political turmoil and changes of dynasty that had disturbed most great families. However, with the coming of the Hanoverians was a new stability, which allowed the aristocracy to refurbish and improve their houses, and enlarge and develop their estates. There was increased mobility too, and the custom of 'visiting' among polite society flourished. Consequently, competition, as well as a genuine interest in their estates, stimulated estate owners to keep up with their neighbours and seek alternatives in garden design. The time had come to break with formality and the restrictive French style of knots and topiary, straight *allées* and rigid walks. Experimentation led to the grandiose buildings of the ancients, seen on the 'Grand Tour',[1] being emulated in the garden buildings of the landscape parks, which became magnificent arenas of classical grandeur. The love of nature, which satisfied the Romantic instinct, was the spirit of the age. In their fascination with the strange and curious, the Romantics turned to the remote: far-away places, the past, and even the primitive.

Classical architecture did not quarrel with the Romantic view of nature: the wildness of Salvator Rosa, the sylvan landscapes of Poussin, and the Virgilian scenes of Claude Lorrain complemented its grandeur, but there was room for further experiment. England was ready for a change of style, not only in the architecture of the houses, and the design of parks and gardens, but also in the architectural style of garden buildings.

Variety was introduced by using exotic styles from the Far East, and an interest grew up in the capricious and frivolous elements of the gardens of the remote and distant Chinese culture. Accounts of Chinese gardens, brought back by Marco Polo (1256–1323) from the East in the second half of the thirteenth century, had been received in the West as fairy-tales, so far were they removed from Western ideas. However, these tales were confirmed and added to by later traders, travellers, and Jesuit missionaries. Sir William Chambers (1726–1796) returned from China and published works on what he had seen there. People became familiar with the Chinese garden from the scenes frequently found ornamenting imported Chinese porcelain, lacquer-work, and screens. There was a passionate interest in Eastern religions, and gardens thus came to be seen as places for solitude and meditation, as well as theatrical playgrounds of festival and fun. The post-Cromwellian Restoration led to overt sophistication, and the backlash for the luxury-loving society was the appeal of the 'natural'. So, as well as the frivolous elements of Chinoiserie, the thatched and timbered buildings of the Chinese landscape also found a place in the English park, and laid part of the foundation for 'the rustic taste'.

'Dreaming of Immortality in a Thatched Cottage', detail of a sixteenth-century painting by Chou Chen

The eighteenth-century arrival of the ballad, historical fiction, and the new poetry of nature appealed to the European imagination. In 1719, Daniel Defoe (1660–1731) wrote *The Life and Surprising Adventures of Robinson Crusoe of York*, who was shipwrecked, and found himself alone on the uninhabited island of Oroonoque. Forced to live in a state of nature (well, almost, for he was allowed the luxury of screws and saws), he built himself a bower in the countryside.

There was a fashionable interest in the primitive life of the 'noble savage'. In 1755, a second edition of *Essai sur l'architecture*, by the French theorist, Abbé Laugier, was published; the frontispiece was an illustration of a primitive hut made with rough branches.

Sir William Chambers, a fashionable author after his work at the royal gardens at Kew, not only spoke of 'the miserable huts'[2] of China in his writings on gardens, but went on, in *A Treatise on the Decorative Part of Civil Architecture* (1759),[3] to describe three versions of the primitive hut in the evolution of architecture: the first was a conical branch hut; the second, a rectangular building formed with tree trunks for columns (rather like Laugier's primitive hut); and the last, a building of proto-Doric columns. However, whereas Chambers was concerned with the evolution of architecture, Laugier's primitive hut was born of his Romantic ideals, that he associated with a 'Golden Age', and a closeness to nature.

(Opposite:) Primitive Hut, Abbé Laugier, 1755

The three books mentioned above, in addition to the reports of travellers, no doubt contributed to the intellectual and theoretical debate current during the eighteenth century, and helped to popularize the rustic style that became a feature of the landscape park. Elements of the Italian and Chinese garden came together to provide a Romantic landscape, where architecture was an accessory. The rustic style played its part, for as well as being able to stimulate many moods, it remained closely allied to nature. There were many designers ready to show the way, and no shortage of patterns and plans.

Traditional methods and designs had been handed down over the generations by local craftsmen, who had little knowledge of, or communication with the world beyond their own environment and, through lack of stimulation, were often unable to provide new styles. Innovations were left to architects and designers, who had broader social contacts and who might have made the Grand Tour, and who were, therefore, well acquainted with new fashions, and not lacking in inspiration for the creation of fresh designs.

The middle years of the eighteenth century witnessed a glut of pattern books, covering every sort of rustic feature it is possible to imagine in a garden setting: rustic seats, arbours and greenhouses, gates and palings, bridges and bowers, and even libraries and bath houses. It became fashionable to have a rustic building (or two) hidden in your landscape park, and few fashionable parks could not boast a rustic building of some sort, most of which employed the crudest form of construction. The building materials often included flints and irregular stones, but many were built using tree roots, stumps, and branches; the more gnarled and knotty the better. The buildings were frequently thatched, with heather or reeds and a wide variety of rustic decoration embellished the features. Many were built to be used in particular seasons.

Some designers and pattern books, and those rustic buildings that have escaped the ravages of time, are worthy of special attention. Thomas Wright of Durham (1711–1786) started out in life as a clockmaker, before becoming a sailor and then a teacher of mathematics. He later became tutor to the children, grandchildren and other relatives of the Duke and Duchess of Kent, teaching astronomy, drawing, mathematics and surveying:[4] all important matters for 'gentlemen of taste'. However, his career then took yet another turn, this time to architecture and garden design.

Wright went to work at Badminton, and the fourth Duke and Duchess of Beaufort

(Opposite:) 'The Upright and Plan of a Stibadium, or Arbour of the Tholus Kind, proposed for Entertainments in the open Air', Thomas Wright, 1755.
'This Building in some Measure approaches to regular Architecture, and is designed for the Center of a Rosery [sic] or Plantation of Shrubs, verged round with an ever-green screen, it is supported upon eight Poles, or may rest upon Lattice Frames cover'd with Jessamin as high as the Cornice, which has a Palladian Projection, i.e. equal to the whole Entablature, in order to carry off the Wet from the Roof, which may be Canvas well oiled and painted. The Head on the Apex is a four faced Janus, representing the Year, and the Busto's on the impost are designed to represent the Months, the Apertures in the Frize, and the Corona on the Roof may be decorated with artificial Ivy, Honey-suckles, Pine-apples, Green and Grey Moss, &c. to the Builder's Fancy. The Ground Work may be Turf or Sand'

were instrumental in the publication of his *Universal Architecture*, one of the first works on rustic garden architecture. The first volume, *Six Original Designs for Arbours* (1755) was subscribed to by relatives and family friends of the Beauforts, and enjoyed considerable success. Alas, Mr Wright's mind was 'elsewhere, on celestial subjects out of the common track of human affairs'.[5] His preoccupation with scientific interests left little room for the promotion of his books, and the second volume, *Six Original Designs for Grottoes* was, sadly, a dismal failure.

Nevertheless, although reputed to be an eccentric, Wright was both generous and humorous, a man of knowledge and imagination. No doubt a charismatic personality, he enjoyed continuous support from influential and powerful friends throughout his life and designed numerous gardens and garden buildings for the aristocracy.[6]

The engraved designs in Wright's books, which probably depict designs for specific patrons, are superbly executed, and attractively enhanced by complete landscape settings. Wright was another Romantic spirit and his writings show that he shared a common philosophy with the French theorist, Abbe Laugier:

> In general, great Precautions will be necessary with Regard to the Situation of the Designs, that no one of them appear in Sight of another or of any Regular Piece of Architecture, being imagined to please most where they may naturally be supposed the only Productions of the Age, before building became a Science.[7]

In his descriptive yet succinct text, he goes on to describe the method of construction of his buildings and, as well as recommendations on their siting, he provides suggestions for the kind of floor or ground cover, ornament, and climbing plants. The two most attractive garden buildings in Wright's book are, perhaps, 'The Stibadium, or Arbour of the Tholus Kind, proposed for Entertainment in the Open Air' and the 'Ornithon or Aviary'.

Aviaries and menageries, where birds and animals were kept as spectacles of curiosity, were a common feature of eighteenth-century landscape parks. A menagerie was built at the Jardin des Plantes, Paris, in 1794, and several other French provincial cities followed suit. It became the custom to have animal houses built in the rustic style, and this style of architecture still remains in French zoological gardens. Some of the modern designs follow early patterns, and others have been built or decorated by gardeners or keepers who have used their own creative abilities.

(Opposite:) 'The Elevation and Plan, of an Ornithon, or Arbour of the Aviary Kind, chiefly contrived for the Reception of singing and other beautiful Birds', Thomas Wright, 1755.
'The Manner of Executing this design is with the rugged Trunks of Oak, the more fantastical and robust the better, the Architrave or Eve-band is of the same unhewn Material, and supports a like rude Cornice, in some Degree reduced to Order and Design, with large and prominent regular Nobs instead of Modillions; the Roof is thatched, and of a Roman pitch, with a Palladian Projection, and to render it still more secure of Shade and Shelter, it may be enclosed on three Sides at least, or five at most, being principally constructed for a Point of View, and to command a large Extent of the Horizon; on the Inside it may be fitted up and finished with Ivy-Flakes and Moss, or otherwise with the roughest Bark of Oak, variagated and comparted with Knots, yet so as to appear all of one Mass growing together by the Consent of Nature. The Floor may be either Sand, Gravel, or Pebbles agreeable to the Builder's Fancy'

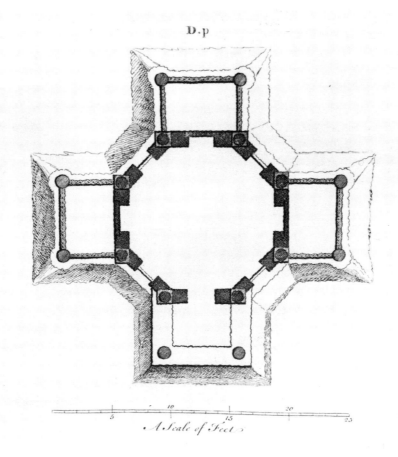

D.p

A Scale of Feet

Cabanes du Jardin des plantes.

Cabanes du Jardin des plantes, Roret, c.1840. Animal houses for French Zoological Gardens have traditionally been constructed in rustic-work

Decorative motifs frequently adorn rustic buildings, and in the eighteenth century they were usually symbolic: skulls and crooked crosses, tablets engraved with mottoes and inscriptions, and fruit or flowers. Thomas Wright of Durham embellished his 'Hovel', designed for solitude, with an owl, to nurture wise thought. His 'Arbour of the Tholus Kind proposed for Entertainment in the Open Air', was elaborately decorated. The embellishments often reflect Thomas Wright's scientific interests and intellectual vein of thought.

Wright's garden buildings were all different from each other, and were roofed with different materials. The Stibadium had a painted canvas roof, but the Ornithon had a thatched roof.

Thatching is one of the oldest building crafts, and possesses an enduring romantic appeal. The same tools and materials have been used for centuries. The materials have, in the past, varied according to what was grown locally: water reed, *Phragmites communis*, grown mainly in Norfolk, but nowadays frequently exported from Austria, is without question the favourite, because it grows very tall, sometimes up to a height of 10 feet. Although water-reed thatch is very expensive, it should last about 60 years if properly maintained, and some roofs are known to have lasted over 100 years.

The life of straw thatch is shorter, but, because it has always been very readily available, its use has been widespread. Heather, too, because of its availability, was once a popular choice for thatching, but it is now mainly used in Scotland and Cumbria. However, a long-lasting heather thatch (in contrast to the amateur method mentioned in Chapter 1) is a skilled job, and if not done properly will soon allow water to penetrate.

The charm of thatch never fades. It provides excellent insulation, keeping garden buildings snug and cosy in winter and cool in summer. Nevertheless, there are a few points to remember: it is better not to site a thatched garden building under trees, as this will encourage the growth of moss, and fallen leaves may build up on it. Birds are sometimes a nuisance and will attack straw, particularly if grains of wheat are still present, but more of a problem are squirrels, as they may burrow into a thatched roof to make a store for their winter hoard of nuts. A covering of fine wire netting will protect against this, and also give some protection against moss (and it is not very obvious). Fortunately, if a hole is made by squirrels, it can be easily repaired.

A modern rustic animal house, le Jardin des Plantes, Paris

A summerhouse floor of knapped flints and horses' molars

Fire is no longer considered the hazard it once was, and in a garden building a fire is even less likely than in a house. Straw and reed can be treated to become fire-resistant and, recently, a new material for lining a thatched roof has been developed, tested, and proved to be very successful in preventing fire.

At Spetchley Park, Worcestershire, one of Thomas Wright's thatched rustic buildings still stands. Thomas Wright is known to have visited Worcester in the 1760s and the engraved design of the frontispiece of *Six Designs for Arbours* is distinctly the 'Root House' built at Spetchley Park. This sturdy little summerhouse is one of the best surviving examples of Wright's garden buildings. It measures only 10 feet across and 15 feet high, is constructed on a foundation of roots and tree stumps, and has a thatched roof supported by eight pillars of knobby and deformed elm. (The park at Spetchley was once noted for its fine avenues of elm trees, but, unfortunately, these were felled in the early 1970s when Dutch elm disease took its toll.) The interior of the little hut is decorated with twig-work of diamond and diagonal patterns, and matching built-in rustic benches stand upon a cobbled floor (Plate 9).

(Opposite:) Herringbone-patterned brick path in the flower garden at Parnham House, Beaminster, Dorset

Thomas Wright suggested turf, stone pavement, gravel, sand, pebbles, and horses' teeth as being suitable surfaces for the floors of his garden buildings. Mosaics of horses' teeth, and sheep's and deer's knuckle-bones were frequently used to form the floors of garden buildings, and at West Dean, Sussex, a design of knapped flints and horse's molars was used as late as 1911 for the floor of the gazebo. Knapped flints were traditionally a common feature of the architecture around Sussex.

Pebbles or cobbles have been used world-wide as a method for paving for centuries, but perhaps the oldest reference is Ji Cheng's *Yuan ye* (Garden Decoration), the standard work on Chinese garden construction, published during the Ming period (1368–1644). A variety of patterns were used in the gardens of Suzhou and some can still be seen today (Plate 10).

> Inside buildings floors were of square bricks but in walkways these square bricks were often laid on their sides and arranged in geometric patterns. All sorts of floors are found, crazy paving, stone slabs, pebbles, broken bricks and broken porcelain set in 'flower paths'. In construction, the ground was first hammered flat then covered with a 5 mm layer of sifted earth in which the patterns in stone, brick, tile and so on were laid.[8]

Traditional paths of brick laid in a herringbone pattern look very attractive in a rustic garden, but pretty paths can be made up using a variety of collected pieces that will add considerable interest, and perhaps contribute to a volume of memories. At Fanhams Hall, Hertfordshire, one flower garden has a network of brick paths, with coats of arms, a picture of the house, a windmill, and various other symbols worked into them.

The summerhouse at Spetchley has an open front, with small, ogee-shaped openings on either side, which may once have been glazed with a lattice of coloured glass. Diamond-shaped window panes are a legacy of the days before glass, when, to keep intruders at bay, windows were filled with lattices of cleft oak laths. The diagonal arrangement also encouraged raindrops to run downwards rather than to form drips that could be blown into the room.

It is often difficult to imagine how a garden looked in earlier times, but it is known that Thomas Wright's garden schemes were highly commendable. Sylvan spinnies were decorated with roses; winding paths led to open glades; woods were divided into garden rooms, and seats were placed against a background of shrubs.[9]

The park at Spetchley has changed little since Wright's time, but the garden has received constant attention and alterations have been made by successive generations of the Berkeley family. Rose Berkeley, with the help of her sister Ellen Willmott, famous for her own garden at Warley Place in Essex, made Spetchley and Edwardian plantsman's paradise. Those who have come after her have continued in the same vein, cherishing and caring for this centuries-old garden.

The old Horse Pool, where once horses paused to drink after a long journey, is now surrounded by magnolias and hydrangeas, and two Judas trees, *Cercis siliquastrum*, stand each side of the water. The Melon Yard is a haven for tender plants, and here the yellow flowers of the *Cytisus battandieri* give their pineapple scent. The mixed borders, with their old-fashioned roses, paeonies, irises and mulleins, spill out on to the garden paths.

In the spring there are masses of flowering bulbs: *Narcissus jonquilla* grow among the roses, and carpets of *Crocus tomasinianus* and *Fritillaria meleagris* grow beneath the branches of the scarlet oak *Quercus coccinea* 'Splendens'.

There is a superb collection of trees and the diarist John Evelyn mentioned one of the cedars. A magnificent specimen of tree paeony, *Paeonia lutea* 'Souvenir de Maxime Cornu', was obtained by Ellen Willmot from the Royal Gardens at Peking, and the *Rhus verniciflua* is the tree that yields the varnish used in Japanese lacquer. The Cork Lawn takes its name from a gnarled specimen of the cork tree, *Quercus suber*, growing there, and close by, beside the stream that wanders away from the Garden Pool, is the little summerhouse, its knobbly piers competing with the contorted roots of the nearby *Taxodium distichum* (known as the 'Knobbly Knee' tree). The plants around the summerhouse add to its charm: bamboos, towering above, rustle in the breeze; the crowns of the shiny-leaved mahonias are decorated with yellow beads, and ferns spill on to the gravel paths. Bulrushes grow in the nearby stream and these, together with the fir tree, are the traditional requisite to accompany every eighteenth-century summerhouse.

Another quaint garden building can be found in Berkeley, Gloucestershire, a small Georgian town dominated by a formidable castle (Plate 11). This little hut, of *c*.1790, was designed for Edward Jenner by his friend the Reverend Robert Ferryman, and still stands in the garden of what is now the Jenner Museum.

Edward Jenner was a country doctor born in Berkeley in 1749, and known world-wide as the 'Father of Immunology'. He was the son of the Vicar of Berkeley and, after studying at St George's Hospital, London, returned to his native town. He contributed to papers on heart disease, recorded one of the earliest accounts of hypothermia, and became the country doctor at Berkeley.

Jenner was a man of his time; in this age of 'Enlightenment', when other folk were returning to a romantic appreciation of nature, his interests were more practical; his delight was in the serious study of nature. As well as helping to launch a hydrogen balloon, he studied the hibernation of hedgehogs, and published a paper on the natural history of the cuckoo. Today, however, he is remembered for his discovery of vaccination, by proving that injections of the cowpox virus produced immunity against smallpox.

Jenner loved his home, 'The Chantry', which stands between the church and Berkeley Castle, and in the grounds is the rustic thatched hut that he called the 'Temple of Vaccinia', and in which he vaccinated the poor people of Berkeley. Some say he used the local villagers for his experiments, but whatever his purpose, he made no charge, and his success cannot be measured, for he ranks among the greatest benefactors to mankind.[10]

Jenner was fond of his garden, which remains much the same as it was in his day. In the vinery there still grows a grape vine planted by Jenner. It is said to have been grown from a cutting taken from a plant in Esssex which was also the parent of the famous vine at Hampton Court (the sixteenth-century home of the English Cardinal Wolsey). Jenner's tiny thatched hut stands in a far corner of the garden, in the shadow of the church in whose graveyard he lies buried. It has a single room and it is brick-built, but the brickwork is disguised, inside and out, by a decorative conglomeration of untrimmed, knobbly tree trunks, giving the rusticated look so popular in the eighteenth century.

Brick paths at Fanhams Hall, Ware, Hertfordshire

Ornamental Architecture in the Gothic, Chinese and Modern Taste, by Charles Over, was published in 1758, and contained more than 50 'Intire New Designs of Plans, Sections and Elevations'. These designs were suitable for 'Gardens, Parks, Forests, Woods and Canals'; five of them are for timber buildings; and four are constructed with tree roots. The features made from roots are particularly interesting, and the appearance of root structures in Charles Over's pattern book may, perhaps, confirm the influence of the Chinese landscape on the English garden. From the 1750s to the 1760s 'rustic' was considered to be a Chinese style, and only later was it thought of as part of English rural vernacular architecture. Some of Charles Over's designs display a Chinese influence, and particular references to Chinese designs are seen in a rusticated archway, formed from tree roots and stated to be in a style 'much used by the Chinese'[11] to frame a view; and also in a design for a footbridge that is decorated with tree roots. Garden structures and sophisticated root furniture were popular features in Chinese gardens, and furniture formed from roots can be found in scenes decorating antique Chinese porcelain. Items constructed from roots are still sold at the annual Canton Fair.

Decoration with tree roots is very effective, as roots are often very interesting shapes in themselves and are usually more pliable than branches. Decorative pieces of tree roots were sometimes secured to a plainer construction — an easy way to transform a simple hut or bridge, and to give gnarled branches an even more grotesque appearance.

An enchanting little book by William Wrighte, published in 1767, has the title *Grotesque Architecture; or, Rural Amusement*, which sums up the eighteenth-century craze for rustic garden buildings. Indeed, most garden conceits at this time were intended for rural amusement, and the book contains a large selection of brief plans for the construction of fanciful rustic pleasure-houses, products of the wildest imagination, where one could indulge in a variety of activities.

The frontispiece of this delightful book depicts a landscape park complete with ruins, a circular building decked with flags flying high on their poles, and a root house. Labourers and hermits, gentleman and surveyor, are diligently going about their tasks of building the various grotesque architectural features. This is certainly a frontipiece that would encourage any gentleman keen to partake of 'Rural Amusement', and to get into the swing of things with the 'moving of earth'. There is a design for a 'Primitive Hut', built from 'Trunks of Trees and Irregular Timber', lined with moss and covered with thatch, and based on the design for a primitive hut designed by Sir William Chambers. Another 'Rural Amusement' is a design for a 'Grotesque or Rural Bath, very proper to be built in Gardens &c. for the Benefit of Bathing'. This jolly looking structure is shaped like a giant beehive, and sports a flamboyant decoration of thistle and grasses protruding from the top. Inside are three seats included for 'the conveniency of dressing and undressing', and a circular bath is positioned in the centre.

In eighteenth-century England, 'taking the waters' and bathing became very popular and as well as enjoying the waters at spa towns, which were made famous by these

(Opposite:) This frontispiece from Grotesque Architecture; or, Rural Amusement, *William Wrighte, 1767 shows landowner, surveyor, and hermit improving a landscape park*

FRONTISPIECE.

A. Thornthwaite inv.   Isaac Taylor sculp.

Where Severn, Trent, or Thames's Ouzy side   The Moss, or gliding Streams productive Store,
Pours the smooth Current of their easy Tide,   To grace the Building on the Verdant Shore,
Each will require a sameness to the Spot,   There the rough Tuscan, or the Rustic fix't,
For this a Cell, a Cascade or a Grot: Or Pebbles, Shells, or calcin'd Matter mix,
The frozen Isicles resembled form,
Or Sea-green Weed your Grotto must adorn.

Art of Architecture, a Poem.

Grotesque, or Rural Bath.

The grotto and bandstand at Chatsworth, Derbyshire

pursuits, some landed gentry had plunge pools or bath houses constructed in their gardens or parks. The idea was not new: there are remains of baths dating from Roman and medieval times, but in the eighteenth century the fashion for bathing enjoyed a revival.

An interesting comparison with Wrighte's bath house is 'The Men's Bath House', a woodcut by Albrecht Dürer (1497). An unusual subject, and unknown before this date (although this is not to say that such places did not exist previously), the bath house depicted is an open, rustic building, and the scene is clearly a light-hearted social occasion, complete with musician. However, only one's own imagination can decide whether Wrighte's bath house was for the benefit of the bather's health or a 'Rural Amusement'!

Grottoes were found in many ancient gardens, in both the Far East and the Western world, and, later, frequently featured in the landscape park and the rustic garden. In ancient Greece they were honoured as the domain of nymphs and muses; in Italy they

(Opposite:) Grotesque or Rural Bath, Grotesque Architecture; or, Rural Amusement, *William Wrighte, 1767*

were underground 'rooms', providing an elaborately decorated refuge from the heat of the day, and in ancient China, they provided a cool cave-temple for meditation, where the walls were decorated with Chinese scenes.

Numerous grottoes of antiquity have been unearthed, and they are nearly always elaborately decorated. The ornamental plants, animals, and human figures of ancient Italian grottoes became known as *grotesques*. During the Italian Renaissance, the style was frequently imitated by the famous artists, Ghirlandaio, Pinturichio and Raphael, and these grottoes became places of fun and frolic, where water jokes usually played a part in the entertainment. Shells, ores, minerals, and even semi-precious stones, all have been used to decorate grottoes since the eighteenth century, when, perhaps with the advent of the new fairy tale of Aladdin, they were built in imitation of his cave.

In a secluded corner, near the southern end of the grounds of Chatsworth House, Derbyshire, there is a grotto that was designed by White Watson, the Bakewell geologist, who was paid the sum of £66.18s.6d for his 'time and trouble in designing the grotto and for fossils'. The grotto was built for Lady Georgiana Spencer (1757–1806), wife of the 5th Duke of Devonshire, who was a collector of crystals, and in 1844, her son, the 6th Duke, wrote:

> The grotto was built by my mother; and I respected its exterior when the addition was made of a natural cavern, formed of crystals of copper ore that were discovered in Ecton mine, on the borders of Staffordshire, and had to be removed in the hope of finding some of the lost side veins. Vain hope! the produce ceased to repay the labour of the works, instead of amounting, as it is said to have done in the one year, to the sum of £300,000 – a fortunate God-send, that paid for the building of Buxton Crescent, and I should hope for a great deal besides. The crystals are curious, because they contain the ore, instead of being, as is usual, encrusted by it.[12]

Rustic features were often used in conjunction with grottoes, and the Chatsworth grotto is made more interesting by the addition of a rustic bandstand, which was built at a later date to sit prettily on top of the grotto. The bandstand, reached by a flight of steps threading their way through the trees, has a splendid view out over the 'Grotto Pond'. This ancient fish-pond is surrounded by a splendid variety of specimen trees collected over the years, and a succession of wild flowers grow among the long grass. How romantic it must have been to picnic here and listen to the music wafting across the still water.

Although it is not known for certain when the bandstand was added, the account book of 1820 notes that Sampson Newton was paid £12.5s.6d. for watching at night to prevent 'depradations'.[13] Unfortunately, times do not change, and although one can climb the steps and enjoy the view from the bandstand, the interior of the cavern is now kept locked.

3
HERMITS AND HERMITAGES

No pattern book of garden buildings was complete without one or two designs for an ornamental hermitage. No more than a hovel, built using a framework of tree trunks infilled with a conglomeration of roots and gnarled and knotty branches, and roofed with a thatch of straw, reeds or heather; this was home for the professional, ornamental hermit. Paid to dress in coarse cloth, wear a rosary of dried peas, and goat-like beard, and to lead an eremitical life, his only comforts were a bed of straw and some crude rustic furniture. This way of life was a morbid charade, but a great source of amusement to visitors to the landscape park, who came to marvel at this weird, yet wonderful spectacle.

It is difficult to decide exactly what inspired the craze for ornamental hermitages or, indeed, the 'ornamental' hermits who inhabited them, but there they were, set up by men of culture and fortune as part of the scenery of the landscape park. We can only speculate upon the influences which promoted their popularity: hermits were not unknown in England, at one time their huts were often seen in the English countryside, close to fords, and their blessings were valued by devout travellers. Some hermits took care of roads and bridges as a religious duty, and could be authorized to collect a toll for their trouble. King Edward III gave official permission to William Philippe, a hermit who lived north of London, to collect a toll 'from our people passing between Heghgate and Smethfelde', to pay for repairs of the Hollow Way.[1]

There were, of course, solitary religious hermits such as those of the Carthusian Order. These were the 'gardening monks' who lived in the Charterhouses, each cultivating his own patch of garden at the back of his cell, whilst leading a life of silence and seclusion. Perhaps the Carthusian's little plot was like a Muslim prayer carpet: a sacred space, where, isolated from everyday life, he could ascend in harmony with his prayer to a higher celestial plane.

A general interest in the religions of the Far East and in the 'miserable huts'[2] of China, inhabited by ascetics, may well have contributed to hermitages being used as ornaments. The great Chinese painter gardener Chang Seng-Yu, of the sixth century, described a retreat of a philosopher-poet who found conditions more congenial in the countryside.

> The thatched cottage for the resident philosopher-hermit was set among the trees at the foot of a mountain; there was a stream, a lily pond, some chrysanthemums, a few fruit trees grown for their blossom, an old and preferably gnarled pine, perhaps a clump of bamboo and some fantastic rocks.[3]

These influences may all have played a role in promoting the vogue for ornamental

Bridges for a hermit, Johan Grohmann, 1796

hermitages. The Romantic spirit was nurtured by focusing upon nature and the natural rather than the material things of life, and perhaps stressed the importance of space and time necessary for self-reflection and melancholy meditation upon the humble inner-self.

It would have been rare for an estate owner to become a recluse, but his patronage of a hermit may have represented his awareness of the importance of nature, and displayed to the world that, given the time and opportunity, this was how he would like to spend his life!

Eighteenth-century ornamental hermitages were almost always in a solemn and sequestered place, in the shadow of a forest with water running nearby. William Wrighte, author of *Grotesque Architecture; or, Rural Amusement*, suggested his 'Augustinian Hermitage' should be 'built on a small verdant Amphitheatre near a murmuring stream',[4] and the designer Charles Over required his hermitage should be

> ...raised not more than Six Feet, and placed in some large cavern or adjoining to craggy impending Rocks; it must not be destitute of sweet water...[5]

Contemporary interest in primitive architecture and the 'Noble Savage' also played a part in developing the fashion for hermitages as part of the trend for the love of nature, and it was essential that the hermitage was constructed with local materials, nothing exotic, and that it should look as if built by the hermit himself. The roof was often thatched with heather, sometimes as an ornamental layer on top of a straw base. Heather used for thatching is gathered while still in bloom but it has a tendency to turn black and is sometimes despised as being dreary. However, this would make it most suitable for a sombre hermitage.

Frequently, a skull and crooked cross adorned the ornamental hermitage. The energy of the crucifix was said to annul the demonic power of grottoes. Other decorations were owls, or tablets with an inscription. So much the better if the inscription was in Arabic, for this would lend an air of mystery.

The first ornamental hermitage was probably 'Merlin's Cave', built at Richmond by William Kent (1685–1748) for Queen Caroline. Here lived Stephen Duck, a Wiltshire farmworker-cum-poet who, in addition to being the Royal Thatcher, became Keeper of the Queen's hermetic retreats. It was his duty to play the role of ornamental hermit and guide to visitors. However, Duck rose in station to become Poet Laureate. By strange coincidence he later held an honorary position created by Charles II as Governor of Duck Island in St James' Park! It is also said that Duck was at one time Rector of Byfleet.

An engraving shows the building was not in the rustic timber style, but nevertheless full of wit and humour, with three, conical thatched roofs giving it the appearance of a group of haystacks. There were leaded lights to throw sunshine upon the rustic interior of this quaint fairyland cottage; rustic bookcases, formed from natural branches, housed Mr Duck's library, and their design complemented the structural piers which supported a groined roof in rustic-gothic style. There was an air of mystery and magic about the place, for Mr Duck shared his home, which was decorated with astrological symbols, with some unusual guests. These comprised waxwork figures of Minerva, Queen Elizabeth and her muse, and the Wizard Merlin, who was chief, and his secretary.[6] Unfortunately, all were swept away when Capability Brown re-landscaped

Section of Merlin's Cave complete with rustic bookcases. Built in 1735 by William Kent in Richmond Gardens for Queen Caroline, to house Stephen Duck and his library

the Royal Gardens at Richmond and, in 1772, in *An Heroic Epistle*, William Mason gave his opinion of this deed in no uncertain terms:

> ...Come then, prolific Art, and with thee bring
> The charms that rise from thy exhaustless spring;
> To Richmond come, for see untutor'd Brown
> Destroys those wonders which were once thy own.
> Lo, from his melon-ground the peasant slave
> Has rudely rush'd, and levell'd Merlin's Cave;
> Knock'd down the waxen Wizard, seiz'd his wand,
> Transform'd to lawn what late was Fairy land;
> And marr'd, with impious hand, each sweet design
> of Stephen Duck, and good Queen Caroline...[7]

William Kent went on to work at Badminton, and he may have been working there at the same time as Thomas Wright of Durham, who designed the hermitage in the forest.[8] The forest is now gone, but the hermitage, completed by October 1747, is one of the last to survive.

When the strange and grotesque hermitage began to rise in the forest at Badminton, choice trees were felled and their knotty trunks used to form the corner-posts of this curious little building. Grotesque lintels and pedimented ends were put into place, and the framework of this hermit's cell, measuring 20 × 24 feet, was complete. This was no ordinary building, for the framework was packed tightly with a solid mass of rough roots and gnarled branches to form the walls, just as Thomas Wright recommended for other hermitages, in his *Universal Architecture*:

> ...and is finished without, with the rough Knots, and Pertuberances of Oak, closely connected together, the Waste-work of the Inside and also the Cove or Ceiling is altogether one close texture of Ivy Thrums, and mixed with Moss, Green below the Eve board and Grey above it.[9]

All is protected by a thatch of straw, which once rose to form a turret at the centre. A huge forked branch was inverted to create the door frame and, at the rear, there is an arch formed of rustic timbers where once two rustic chairs stood. The chairs have long since been replaced by a bench in the rustic style, but the inscription, worked in

The Badminton hermitage, composed of a conglomeration of gnarled and knotty tree roots, branches, and trunks

The seat at the rear of Badminton hermitage

nailheads up one side of the branch and down the other, remains: 'Here loungers loiter — Here the weary rest.'

The interior decoration of the single, almost Palladian-style room of the Badminton hermitage has, surprisingly, remained very much intact, and remnants of dried moss still line the ceiling and sides of the alcove. Where the moss has fallen, the carpenter's pencil marks can still be seen.[10] What remains is sadly in need of attention and care, but only the imagination can tell us how it might have looked when the moss was fresh and green, and the building filled with chunky rustic furniture.

The Badminton hermitage may have had an additional use, for marked out on the wooden floor are a series of mathematical problems — further evidence of Mr Wright. Unfortunately, an inscription explaining the figures has since disappeared.[11] Mottoes and inscriptions are said to have been part of the original embellishment, and over the entrance to the hermitage there was another inscription:

Obscurum Verborum ambrage novorum,
Urganda heic Carmen Magico demurmurat Ore
English'd: Here Urganda in words dark and perplex'd
Inchantments mutters with her Magic voice.[12]

Although there is no record of a resident hermit, on one wall there is still a faint trace of a picture of Urganda, the wise Enchantress, who was represented with her attendant 'at an altar performing some solemn act of enchantment.' Inscribed on the frame were the words *Magico Lustrabere Ritu* (you shall be purified by Magic Rite).[13]

This was an age when astronomy and astrology were fashionable, and worthy of study at University. 'Enlightened' gentlemen dabbled in the occult and there were mysterious happenings in high circles. Does this mean that the Badminton hermitage had a secret to hide?

Trends were set by people like Sir Francis Dashwood, who founded his secret society, the Hell Fire Club, at Medmenham Abbey. Everyone loves to hear of rogues, and, indeed, Sir Francis and his 12 apostles (or the monks of Medmenham) were decidedly a gang of rogues — so stories of their dark deeds have lived on. At Medmenham, orgies were held, the occult practised, and the Black Mass celebrated. The group were said to be anti-Pope. The Abbey was lavishly decorated and the grounds laid out with temples, statuary and 'cosy nooks' conducive to the romantic adventures of the 'monks' and 'nuns'. The inscriptions, both in the abbey and on columns in the woods, were rather unusual, for they were engraved in bastardized Latin, and their translation was open to interpretation. When the secret of Medmenham became known, Sir Francis had caves specially excavated and sumptuously decorated at his home at West Wycombe, and meetings were then held there. The gardens, too, are said to have been of an extraordinary design, containing temples, arbours and little rustic bridges, but thereby hangs another tale...

Although one enterprising gentleman, James Altham, later Sir James, of Latton, Essex, had his portrait painted by Salvator Rosa (*c.*1665) whilst symbolically posing as a hermit, complete with trappings and trimmings of skull and copy of the gospels, the vogue for hermits and hermitages in fashionable gardens did not get into full swing until the mid-eighteenth century.

There is a thistle in the foreground of Salvator Rosa's painting, representing vanity: a reminder that man's ambitions can be crushed as effortlessly as a gentle breeze can disperse a calyx. On the right-hand side, time eagerly devours the Belvedere, whilst Hermit Altham treads upon the works of Epicaurus, thus rejecting the Latin motto, *Post Mortem nulla voluptas* (No pleasure exists after death), inscribed on its pages; but he looks with relief upon the ascetic text *Post mortem summa voluptas* (The greatest pleasure comes after death).[14]

One cannot help wondering whether the idea of hermit and hermitage, along with some of the more grotesque Italian grottoes, was treated as an early equivalent of today's theme parks; perhaps we may equate the reaction of the eighteenth-century visitor with how we would react to such a sight today. The eighteenth-century imagination was nurtured on ghost stories, fairy-tales, and ballads of romantic glamour; scenes of violence and horror were not an everyday occurrence, as made commonplace by today's television and national press. Perhaps the hermit in his hovel, complete with long beard and rosary of dried peas, inspired the same reaction as a 'ghost train' or 'haunted house' does today: a spectacle to be enjoyed by the visitor, who must endeavour to overcome a ripple (albeit pleasurable) of fear.

Problems with keeping hermits sometimes occurred, but, probably, for an ordinary hardworking peasant, the idea of being provided with a retreat, complete with 'food from the house', as well as monetary reward, was not to be sneezed at, and as well as gentlemen advertising for an ornamental hermit, there were even advertisements of aspiring hermits, seeking to spend life alone and withdrawn from the world in deed and spirit. This was no short-lived fashion and as late as 1810 an advertisement appeared in the *Courier* (11 July):

> A young man, who wishes to retire from the world and live a life of an hermit, in some convenient spot in England, is willing to engage with any nobleman or gentleman who may be desirous of having one. Any letter directed to S. Lawrence (post paid) to be left at Mr OTTON'S, No 6. Coleman's Lane, Plymouth, mentioning what gratuity will be given, and all other particulars, will be duly attended.[15]

However, although there were men anxious to take on such a job, there were few who stayed the course, for there were demands made upon them which even the most worthy could not live up to.

The Hon. Charles Hamilton of Painshill, Cobham, built a hermitage, upon a mound, in the more gloomy depths of his beautiful grounds (as well as many other wondrous features). The building had an upper apartment supported in part by contorted legs and roots of trees and although it is said to have been a 'beautiful retreat', Horace Walpole remarked 'it is the sort of ornament whose merit soonest fades, it being almost comic to set aside a quarter of one's garden to be melancholy in.'[16] However, it was not Charles Hamilton's intention that he himself should be melancholy, and he offered a seven-year contract for a hermit to be melancholy on his behalf. The agreement made the usual demands. He would

> be provided with a Bible, optical glasses, a mat for his feet, water for his beverage and food from the house. He must wear a camlet robe, and never, under any circumstances, must he cut his hair, beard, or nails, stray beyond the limits of Mr Hamilton's grounds, or exchange a word with the servant'.[17]

Lack of conversation, or possibly drink, was this hermit's downfall. He was promised 700 guineas if he remained for seven years. However, if 'driven to madness by intolerable tickling of beard, or scratching of robe [he] broke the conditions: not a penny!'[18] Alas, he was said to have been seen at the local pub after only three weeks!

This poor man was not the only hermit to have given in to worldly distractions and another unfortunate (or perhaps fortunate) fellow was sacked not only for 'certain

Mr Altham as hermit. Salvator Rosa (1615–1673)

'View of the Hermitage in the Vicarage garden, Louth, Lincolnshire', James Bourne (1773–1854)

inappropriate relations with a dairymaid',[19] but for having been caught indulging with a pipe and ale instead of book and beads.

A gentleman near Preston, Lancashire, was anxious to secure the services of a man who would live underground for seven years and, as well as a monetary reward of £50 per annum for life, he was offered some 'rural amusement', for the 'commodious' apartment not only had a cold bath, but also boasted a chamber organ, and as many books as pleased the occupier. Furthermore, there was a bell, which the recluse could ring for any convenience he might require, and provisions were served from the gentleman's own table. This accommodation must have been superior to most, for the successful applicant stayed for four years.[20]

In 1783, at Hawkstone Park in Shropshire, Sir Richard Hill inherited from his father parkland that still remains little known, but is a most striking scenic landscape (Plate 12).

Sandstone hills rise from the North Shropshire Plain and impressive cliffs and rock formations are part of the awe-inspiring magnificence. At the summit of a hill known as 'The Terrace' a spiral staircase with 152 steps leads up to the viewing platform of the Obelisk, erected in memory of the first Sir Rowland Hill. It is said that on a clear day there is a panoramic view over parts of 13 counties.

In spite of the tremendous appeal of this dramatic natural scenery, the entrepreneur Sir Richard Hill set out to 'improve' his landscape still further. As well as forming the two-and-a-half-mile long Hawk Lake, and building numerous follies and a grotto, he even created side-shows. This park became one of the most wondrous and fantastic attractions of its day. It must have enticed many extra tourists to his new hotel, since there was something in the park to appeal to every guest, no matter how diverse their interests. On the famous guided tour one could enjoy not only the thrill and danger of exploring the breathtaking scenery, but also the additional attractions and surprises at every corner; a guide was essential to explore this dangerous terrain to advantage. The tradition of conducted tours was continued by generations of the Jones family. The first Mr Jones was born in 1799 and, at 86 years of age, the present Mr Jones led half-day tours until the late 1980s. The trip to the caves and grotto in Grotto Hill was, and still is, perhaps the visit to the most hair-raising of the features.

Visitors mustered at Gingerbread Hall, so called because there they were served with sweetmeats and gingerbeer, before gathering courage to penetrate a long, deep, and narrow passage, the entrance to a dark tunnel, with no light for some 100 yards. Eventually, the visitor emerges in a labyrinth of caverns. The grotto still has remains of the encrustation of shells, fossils, and other petrifications applied by two Miss Hills in the 1790s, a task that took them over three years to complete. The caverns are lit only dimly by an occasional port-hole window piercing the rock. These openings are said to have been once filled with coloured glass, but now they offer splendid views over the valley. Parts of the passages have no light whatsoever and, groping through the darkness, occasionally one is surprised, and relieved, by a shaft of light, which had been obscured by a bend in the tunnel, piercing the wall of rock.

After this adventure, there was a visit to the hermitage, to be amused by the hermit who, needless to say, was one of the special attractions. The part of hermit was initially played by a pauper, but when Hill was accused of 'slavery', the hermit was replaced by a papier mâché figure. Upon arrival at the hermitage, the visitor pulled a bell to gain entry. In the meantime, the guide, who had sneaked off, rushed around the back to manoeuvre the levers which set this phantasmagoric scene in motion.

Unfortunately, time has taken its toll and vandals have ravaged many of the follies. However, the labyrinth of caverns is still there to be explored, there are many exciting things for the visitor to enjoy, tours are still organized, and the park will soon once again be opened regularly.

There was one very serious hermit, whose achievement was such a work of art that to finish this chapter without telling his story would be tragic.

The Vicar of Louth, in Lincolnshire, was an upright figure of society. Well, almost upright, for although he was elected Town Clerk in 1762 and remained in office until his death, he was accused of never having attended any council meetings. Nevertheless, he loved his parishioners and tended his flock for over 50 years. This unusual character, with flowing black locks and wild eyes, delivered his sermons in such a soft voice they were scarcely audible, but his readings were delivered with gusto and enlivened with his own comments. After the account of the Passion, he is reported to have said 'here endeth that dreadful lesson' and, when he referred to the 'darkness which may be felt' he added 'A thick mist I take it'! Jolland's parishioners found him an eccentric character, but his amiable nature endeared him to all who knew him. He had a large

'View of the Vicarage house from the garden, Louth, Lincolnshire', James Bourne (1773–1854)

following and visitors came to Louth from far and wide; however, it was not to hear him preach that they came, but to admire his vicarage garden.

In the middle of this busy town Vicar Jolland diligently built his garden, complete not only with a hermitage, which was unusual in such a built-up area, but also with many other monuments to his brother, an army man, who had died in India, leaving Jolland a legacy.

The hermitage was surrounded by a garden with neatly trimmed lawns and shrubberies, and a Pavilion with rustic seats in three recesses. More seats and cloisters, all made of tree roots and moss, matched the hermitage. The garden was surrounded by a wall, against which was erected a complete covered way made of trees and thatch, all richly bedecked with roses and creepers. One cloister had pillars formed of timber fancifully covered with the bark of trees and entwined with a profusion of ivy. Saints and apostles carved in wood looked out from the ivy, and there were small windows of stained glass. Beyond the cloisters was an obelisk, and a path shaded by nut and mulberry trees led to another cloister constructed of chalk stone. Crooked arms, made of rough pieces of timber, protruded from the wall as if in wild and grotesque playfulness. Epitaphs, verses and Bible inscriptions were placed in suitable positions around the garden, and in the south-west corner was a 'small alcove denominated 'Shakespeare's Gallery', containing a rustic seat and works of the bard'. North of the hermitage was a herb garden, and the hermit's yard containing a well formed from an old tree trunk.[21]

The completed garden reached full maturity by 1790, when it was visited by Humphry Repton (1752–1818), who made the point that the garden was 'beyond all

I could imagine — it is one of the things which no pen can describe.'[22] Nevertheless, Repton did attempt to describe this extraordinary achievement and wrote a revealing account of the interior of the hermitage, including the hermit's dormitory, which was

> entirely lined by crooked and peeled billets fancifully enriched by knotty excrescences found in the 'unwedg[e]able and knarled oak'. The bed consisted of milk white sheepskins and was raised above the floor so as to require a small staircase to reach it, made of the same kind of billets beautifully clean and polished...suddenly, a part of the wall with the wooden sofa on which I sat, gently moved back, and I found myself in a room somewhat larger and of totally different character![23]

Repton went on to describe the library, which Hermit Jolland described as his brother's library, commenting that what he had taken to be carved wood was, in fact, a collection of the skeletons of leaves and some 'real skeletons of small birds, mice and other little animals...arranged in graceful forms'.

Repton was most impressed with the Chapel and Oratory:

> The effect was magical! It was a fairy tale! Or the Arabian Nights Entertainment! It was all light and no shadow and the light appeared supernatural as it fell upon sparkling gems of every colour...I felt in awe, as if in more immediate presence of the Creator. My eyes moistened as I thought how often the pious Hermit had in this place invoked blessings upon a brother in whom for years every other thought had been absorbed.[24]

Perhaps one of the hermit's most astonishing achievements was his method of decorating walls. Having noticed the glittering trails left by snails, he became determined to avail himself of it, and 'collected hundreds of these little artificers' and with great patience 'directed each little workman in the track he should take'[25] to accomplish his design.

Unlike many, Hermit Jolland included a kitchen as part of the accommodation for the hermitage, and the design betrayed signs that he followed the habits of a recluse of the twelfth century: it looked as though hollowed from rock; the walls were mossy; a lantern was held in a frame of roots; the traditional hermit's hour-glass was supported by fangs; the tinder box was a hollow knot of oak; and there were shells in which to serve food.[26] From this description it must be assumed that Hermit Jolland did spend time at the hermitage as well as, if not instead of, living in the vicarage.

When Jolland died at the age of 85 he was remembered with kindness. All the shops in Louth closed and his funeral was attended by a long train of friends, members of the corporation, 18 clergymen of the town and the children of the national school.[27] Sadly, by 1832 his effects and his collection of memorabilia from the hermitage, including silver and plate, had been sold, and gradually the hermitage and garden fell into neglect and finally, decay.[28] However, there is a lesson to be learned from this story, and perhaps Humphry Repton should have the last word:

> We are all but tenants for life — and if his days were spent in thanksgiving and enjoyment — he might be mad, but he perhaps was less so than many who have passed their lives without either enjoyment or thankfulness.[29]

4

THE PICTURESQUE AND ITS LEGACY

In the late 1700s there was a new vogue for travelling and sketching 'picturesque' scenes in the more rugged parts of England and Wales. The 'Grand Tour' had previously been restricted to the aristocracy. With trouble brewing in France they tended to stay within the British Isles. The ordinary tourist too, now set off on what could be described as a popular version of the Grand Tour. They took with them their easels and sketchbooks (and probably umbrellas) to explore and record the picturesque countryside. But what was meant by the term 'picturesque' and how did it all begin?

The Reverend William Gilpin (1724–1804) has been described as the 'true pioneer of the picturesque'.[1] He grew up in the Border country where he developed a love for the rugged landscape of mountains, rocks and ruins, a love he was later to share with a wide public.

Gilpin was perhaps the most well-known author and draughtsman to take advantage of the new graphic techniques of the day. After his success in publishing his *Essay on Prints*, in which he explained how to examine and appreciate prints, encouraged by his friends, he went on to publish his *Observations* on the sublime, the beautiful, and the picturesque. These volumes were based on his topographical notes and sketches made while travelling through the wilder parts of Wales, around the Lake District, and through the Wye Valley. 'The Mountains and Lakes of Cumberland and Westmoreland' (1786) contained what is no doubt his most quoted statement on the picturesque:

> The horse, in itself, is certainly a nobler animal, than the cow. His form is more elegant; and his spirit gives fire and grace to his actions. But in a picturesque light the cow had undoubtedly the advantage; and is in every way better suited to receive the graces of the pencil.
>
> In the first place, the lines of the horse are round and smooth; and admit little variety: whereas the bones of the cow are high, and vary the line, here and there by a squareness, which is very picturesque. There is a greater proportion also of concavity in them; the lines of the horse being chiefly convex.[2]

These same principles Gilpin applied to the landscape. He considered that 'beauty' described scenes like the landscapes of Capability Brown, with their smooth lawns and neat clumps of trees. 'Picturesque beauty', on the other hand, was more wild and rugged, with roughness of texture, irregularity and even a certain amount of deformity. He admired the irregularities of nature and the rough qualities of brushwood and broken banks. Those trees which were twisted and gnarled with roots exposed, he considered to be features of the picturesque landscape.

However, although William Gilpin himself was not concerned with the picturesque as part of the garden scene, many landscape gardeners were influenced by his ideas. Capability Brown, accused of the impoverishment and disfigurement of the English countryside, was falling out of favour with many people, and one gentleman gardener, Owen Cambridge, had no hesitation in expressing his view. He remarked to Mr Brown that he hoped to die first because, 'I should like to see heaven before you had improved it.'[3] It was towards the picturesque that many landscape gardeners now turned.

Uvedale Price (1747–1829), English landowner and writer, best known for his *Essays on the Picturesque*, brought the picturesque into the garden and, helped by William Sawrey Gilpin (1762–1843), nephew of William Gilpin, he started by developing his own estate at Foxley, near Hereford, in a picturesque style. The younger Gilpin, influenced by Price, became a prominent landscape gardener, often modifying the picturesque by combining it with formal scenes. He went on to design the grounds at Scotney Castle, near Tunbridge Wells, now considered one of the best remaining examples of a picturesque garden. The land at Scotney varies in its levels, so is suited to the intricate and varied picturesque style. Lanes were sunk and stone blasted from the hillside to clear vistas overlooking ruins draped with ivy, or some other nostalgic scene. The planting too, was varied, and many of the trees were new introductions and chosen specially to create a romantic setting.

Scotney Castle. The garden is one of the best remaining examples of a picturesque garden

Rustic features, built with gnarled and knotty branches (sometimes so irregular and deformed they might appear grotesque) became one of the chief elements of the picturesque garden and estate. The quaint qualities of these rustic features contributed to fairy-tale settings and nostalgic scenes.

John Scandrett Harford's mansion, Blaise Castle House was situated not far from the village of Henbury, Avon. It stood on a slightly raised knoll in flat parkland, with hills beyond that dropped into a densely wooded gorge, banked by cliffs. In 1796, Humphry Repton (1752–1818), who gradually came to admire the picturesque, designed a dramatic carriageway for the new mansion. Rather than approach the house by the most direct route across flat ground, his design avoided the village; instead, the route meandered through the rugged countryside, the woodland and around the gorge. 'By cutting away the face of the rock in some places and building lofty walls in others'[4] visitors were given the impression that they were penetrating deep into the countryside. Repton took advantage of the splendid views of the distant mountains, and screened others that he considered insignificant. The route must have been quite hair-raising, particularly in winter, when coaches were swung around hairpin bends as they made the descent on the icy gravelled driveway, before climbing up again to encompass the magnificent views towards the Welsh mountains.

Picturesque rustic architecture was part of the plan for the estate and there is evidence that there was a root house. However, John Nash (1752–1835) took the idea a stage further and designed a dairy with dainty picturesque tendencies, and there is still a timber lodge at the side of the entrance to the drive, attributed to Repton and believed to have been built in the earlier half of the nineteenth century.[5] This quaint building looks quite fragile, but it is deceptively well built, with stone walls that have battens inserted to receive the planks bearing the final covering: an embellishment of gnarled log and twig-work. The effect is of a fairy-tale cottage, from which one feels Little Red Riding Hood might suddenly emerge, wolf hard on her heels! (Plates 13 and 14.)

Estate owners and industrialists became increasingly aware of the advantages of providing comfortable yet ornamental residences for estate workers, which were not only pleasant for the labourer, but also a credit to the estate. Blaise Hamlet, the last of the embellishments to the estate surrounding Harford's Blaise Castle House (1795), was built by him in 1810 to house retired estate workers. It was the first of the estate villages of 'cottages ornées' in the picturesque style. The embellishments include a medley of thatch, lattice-work, twisted chimneys and rustic porches. A centre of attraction then, and now kept neat and trim by The National Trust, Blaise Hamlet is indeed a place to ponder upon.

Old Warden in Bedfordshire was remodelled by Lord Ongley in the mid-nineteenth century. Undeniably attractive, the village resembled a theatrical stage set and it became almost a place of pilgrimage, to which people travelled from far and wide to admire. Some of the cottages have rustic porches, and are decorated with timber. There is a water-pump, under a quaint thatched rustic shelter beneath (Plate 15) which villagers would once have stood to draw their water, clad in the red cloaks and tall

(Opposite:) Thatched tree shelter, the Swiss Garden, Old Warden. This kind of shelter was sometimes known as an 'umbrello' seat

hats made to harmonize with the red-painted doors of their cottages: all part of the picturesque scene insisted upon by Lord Ongley.[6] The garden of the great house covers eight acres, but the intricate design makes it seem much larger. It is picturesque in style, and is believed to have been designed by John 'Buonarroti' Papworth who lived nearby.

The self-styled John 'Buonarroti' Papworth was a talented artist and landscape designer, and doubtless something of an extrovert. Flattered by his brother, who said that his drawing recording the *Victory of Waterloo* had the qualities of Michelangelo, at a ceremony in which two of his friends officiated as High Priests, he took Buonarroti as his middle name! The drawing was submitted to the Royal Academy, but it was not hung. However, he kept the name Buonarroti and became widely known for his ingenious and remarkably attractive designs for all sorts of garden features. Papworth had several important commissions, and became Architect to the King of Wurtemburg.[7]

Now known as 'The Swiss Garden', the park at Old Warden takes its name from the Swiss Cottage standing almost in the centre. This is the focal point of the garden, and is said to have been built by the third Lord Ongley in the 1820s, for his Swiss mistress. Or, it may simply have been part of the rustic fashion sweeping the country. Russian Lodges, Norwegian Hunting Lodges, Canadian Log Cabins, and even Hindoo Huts were not unknown. Whatever it may be, the ornate and enchanting thatched Swiss Cottage still sits, cut into a steep bank, enticing the visitor to climb the steps to its arcaded, circular, rustic porch. The arches are lavishly decorated with twisted twig-work, and a golden filigree of floral and geometrical patterns, embossed with pine-cones and split teazles, lines the canopy. Peering through the window, you see a room, beautifully panelled with fine fretwork, and entered through charming rustic doors. It is here that the family might have enjoyed summer picnics, served to them from the country kitchen that lies concealed below stairs; this can be seen from a lower window at the back of the chalet (Plates 16 and 17).

The garden has now been restored. It is a delightful scene, evoking the romantic ideals of the picturesque. Paths and walks wind their way through shrubbery and woodland, around ponds and across glades, over bridges and under creeper-clad aerial trellises. The meandering paths meet and form a variety of vistas on the way to the many garden features. There is a rock garden, a grotto, a fernery and several rustic conceits. Here, a large oak towers above the simple thatched umbrello that surrounds its huge trunk like a giant mushroom, ready to save the stroller from a sudden shower. There, across the stream, upon a gentle mound, is an 'Indian Kiosk', caressed by the sun pleasantly streaming through its colourful stained-glass window. Lining the thatched, conical roof of the kiosk is a circular ceiling painted with a pattern of rich hues of red and umber, and blue and green. These colours complement the stained glass and rustic roundels, the latter pierced at their centre with a jewel of red glass. Through the three archways at the front is a pleasant view over a pond and across the garden. Last, but not least, amongst the rustic conceits is a pretty little building decorated with logwork, and tucked away in the trees. This is a privy, with an unusual double-seater lavatory! The outdoor privy is now almost a thing of the past (but still quite useful at the back of beyond). Richard and Janet Strombeck have recently designed a pretty little privy with a turf roof. This idea is quite unusual in the west, although habitable buildings with turf roofs are still found in places like Kashmir,

'Northernaire', a privy for the back of beyond. Length: 6 foot; width: 4 foot 8 inches; height: 10 foot 4 inches

where it is not unusual to find sheep grazing above one's head. Norwegian garden and farm buildings of all kinds often have roofs of turf. Traditionally, the turf was laid on top of a roof covering made up of plates of birch bark, but nowadays thick plastic sheeting is spread beneath the turf. The Strombeck's design does not have to be a privy; it could be used as a very attractive garden store, particularly if meadow flowers are allowed to grow in the grass on the roof.

While the new industrialists were using their new riches to embellish their gardens and estate villages, the financial downfall of a number of noble gentlemen was brought about by their colossal expenditure on their parks and gardens. Perhaps one of the most sensational stories was that concerning the picturesque and ornamental garden owned by George Spencer, Marquis of Blandford, who, on the death of his father, became the 5th Duke of Marlborough. This garden was Whiteknights, in Berkshire, and is now the site of the University of Reading. The garden was famed for the ingenious design of its many garden conceits, which are believed to have been the work of John 'Buonarroti' Papworth, although some may have been designed by the Duke himself.

In 1819, Mrs B. Hofland, a novelist, and her husband Sir Thomas C. Hofland RA, who had already painted some fine pictures of Whiteknights, produced a detailed record of the garden and its buildings, comprising charming illustrations, no doubt the work of Sir Thomas, and an enchanting text describing the gardens, written by Mrs Hofland.

The grounds of Whiteknights must have been magnificent, boasting gardens of every description. These included the Botanic Garden and the New Gardens as well as extensive woodlands. Throughout were scattered a splendid variety of rustic greenhouses, garden conceits of the most ingenious designs, complemented by the rich sylvan landscape. The planting schemes were exquisite and flowers of every variety of form, tint, and fragrance, created an unrivalled 'storehouse of Flora'.

There was a broad belt devoted to American plants surrounding the whole grounds; a Japanese Garden, planted entirely with Japanese and American plants, a Rock Garden for alpine plants, and an unusual Striped Garden. This last garden was full of the most

The Diamond Seat, Whiteknights
'This beautiful little Rustic Temple . . . is composed of small branches of Ash, Hazel, and black and white Birch whose shining barks of rich brown and silvery white are worked into a kind of diamond panelling, which is singularly beautiful. The seat is composed of alternate stripes of these contrasted colours, and so contrived as to turn at the edges, and appear at a little distance like a rich scallop fringe.
The roof is supported in the open front by two natural pillars of the Birch tree, round whose fair bark the dark Ivy is beautifully entwined; and though thatched on the outside, is canopied within by branches in the same manner as the sides, and the floor is paved with large and small pebbles, to correspond with the general forms'

curious and beautiful foliage of trees and plants, all of variegated varieties. The oak, ash, box, Spanish chestnut, ivy, and periwinkle were all pied with pure white. The only exception was the cypress tree, which was in strong contrast to the baskets of begonia and China roses encircling it.

The garden conceits were both large and small, simple and intricate and, where appropriate, adorned with a delightful selection of climbing plants. There was a 'Rustic Bower' formed of elm branches in the shape of an alcove, and covered with a fragrant drapery of honeysuckle and jessamin. Branches of trees formed the arch for the three-pinnacled 'Gothic Bower', with plants chosen to bloom in the same season with yellow and light blue flowers. The Temple of Pomona was a greenhouse for collected treasures, 'Never did luxury wear a more inviting aspect, or Contemplation find a softer seat'.[8]

Plate 1 *(Right)* Queen Eleanor's garden, Winchester: the tunnel arbour. A re-creation of a medieval garden, opened by HM the Queen Mother on 8 July 1986.

Plate 2 *(Below)* Wattle fence: inexpensive, pretty, and practical.

Plate 3 *(Above)* Miniature cathedral constructed from willow rods. The Willow Cathedral, Alexander Carse, 1792.

Plate 4 *(Right)* Panels copied from the Willow Cathedral could be used in the construction of summerhouses, or fences, or gates. Drawing believed to be by Edward Blore.

Plate 5 *(Above)* Willow-post bridge, the Alfred McAlpine Garden, RHS Chelsea Flower Show, 1989.

Plate 6 *(Right)* Stream lined with woven willow in the author's Victorian Garden at the RHS Chelsea Flower Show, 1989.

Plate 7 (*Left*) Nesting basket, a pretty addition for pond or lake.

Plate 8 (*Below*) San Anton Garden, Malta. Rustic duck shelters are again becoming popular.

Plate 9 (*Opposite*) The Root House, with knobbly elm piers and twig-work interior. Spetchley Park, Worcestershire.

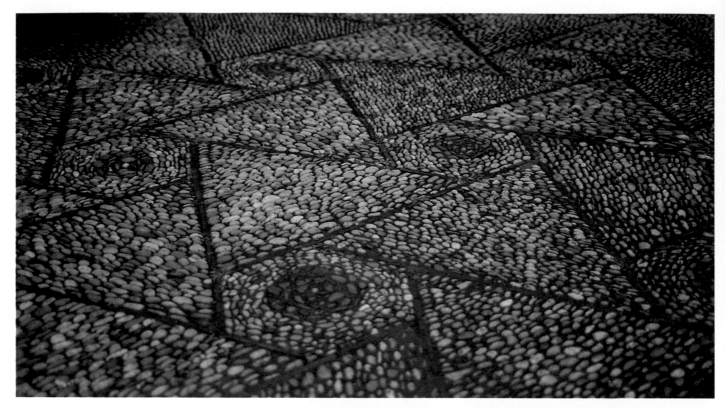

Plate 10 *(Above)* Paving, Suzhou, China. The ground is hammered flat and covered with ½ inch sifted sand in which the patterns of stones or brick are laid.

Plate 11 *(Right)* 'The Temple of Vaccinia' or 'Dr Jenner's Hut', Berkeley, Gloucestershire. It was here that Dr Jenner carried out the first vaccinations against smallpox.

Plate 12   The exit from the labyrinth of man-made tunnels at Grotto Hill,
Hawkstone Park, Shropshire.

Plate 13 *(Above)* Timber Lodge, *c.* 1830, stands by Harford's Drive through Blaise Woods.

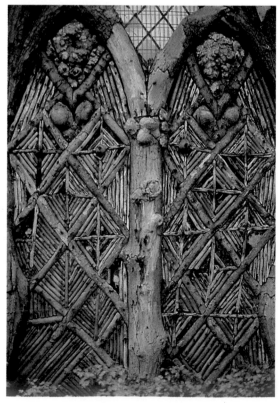

Plate 14 *(Right)* Timber Lodge, detail. The exterior is clad with knots and rods.

Plate 15 Picturesque cottage, Old Warden.

Plate 16 *(Above)* The Swiss Cottage, Old Warden, Bedfordshire. The building is set into a steep bank to provide entrance at both levels. The pyramidal roof extends on all but the north side to form a verandah.

Plate 17 *(Left)* The porch dome of the Swiss Cottage is decorated with twig-work and pine-cones in floral and geometric patterns.

Plate 18 *(Opposite)* Victorian porch at Curload showing mosaic twig-work.

Plate 19 *(Right)* The vaulting of the porch of Rustic Lodge, Kenmore, Perthshire, is a delicacy of diamonds studded with medallions of sawn branches.

Plate 20 *(Below)* The Hermitage, Bicton Park, Devon; a splendid essay on the use of mosaic twig-work and shingles.

Plate 21　Victorian Rustic Garden designed by the author for the RHS Chelsea Flower Show, 1989.

Plate 22 The rustic water pump.

Plate 23 *(Above)* The bridge with larch hand-rails. Twisted by honeysuckle when growing in the wild, they have become 'witch sticks' that repel evil spirits.

Plate 24 *(Right)* The Victorian summerhouse, lined with twig-work and stained glass. The floor was of sawn logs.

Plate 25 (*Above*) Ceiling decoration of the summerhouse.

Plate 26 (*Right*) The Victorian stumpery or fernery.

Plate 27 Rustic flower-basket decorated with mosaic twig-work.

Plate 28 *(Above)*
A garden bench at
Shrubland Park decorated
with ironwork.

Plate 29 *(Left)*
Detail of the swag of
metal leaves.

Plate 30 *(Opposite)*
Railway sleepers edging
a flower-bed.

Plate 31 *(Left)*
Bandstands, bicycles, and rustic-work were all part of the Edwardian scene. View of Hexthorpe Flats, Lancashire.

Plate 32 *(Below)* Rose pergola, Polesden Lacey, Surrey.

Plate 33   Rose pergola, Polesden Lacey, Surrey.

Plate 34 *(Left)* The *whare,* or Maori Meeting House, brought from New Zealand to Clandon Park, Surrey.

Plate 35 *(Below)* The summerhouse in the Kitchen Garden, Ilford Manor Gardens, Wiltshire and Avon. The roof is dutifully supported by a Green Man.

Plate 36 *(Opposite)* View from a summerhouse at West Dean towards the pergola draped with wisteria.

Plate 37 View towards a summerhouse at West Dean. In the foreground is a typical Sussex wall chequered with chalk and knapped flint.

Plate 38 *(Left)* The rustic belvedere was a popular feature in the Jardins Anglais of French parks. Belvedere Rustique, Victor Petit, 1848.

Plate 39 *(Above right)* The hermitage at Frogmore , where Princess Charlotte would spend time studying botany. View by J. Gendall, 1823.

Plate 40 Dr Johnson's summerhouse, Kenwood, Highgate, was carefully
restored but destroyed by fire in May 1991.

Plate 41 *(Right)* William Wordsworth's garden at Rydal Mount, Ambleside, Cumbria.

Plate 42 *(Far right)* A rustic umbrella seat, the RHS Chelsea Flower Show, 1990.

Plate 43 *(Below)* A honey-house on the edge of the New Forest, Hampshire. A useful store for bee-keeping paraphernalia, and a workshop to repair hives, as well as a place to picnic.

Plate 44 *(Above)* The Pavilion, designed by John Adey Repton, 1825, and reconstructed at Scotlands Farm, Wargrave, Berkshire.

Plate 45 *(Left)* A fallen tree trunk in a wild garden can be used to good advantage.

Plate 46 'Willow Lady' woven from willow wands by Madeline Goold.

Plate 47 *(Above)* 'Sidewinder', by Andy Goldsworthy.

Plate 48 *(Left)* The round summerhouse at Furzey Garden, Minstead, has panels of rustic hurdles and is divided into four gossip corners.

Plate 49 *(Opposite)*
This 'Conservationists's Folly' has all mod. cons.

Plate 50 *(Right)* These fences, designed by John Buonarroti Papworth, can be constructed with thinnings or coppiced unbarked wood and fastened together by thongs stripped from other branches. Uprights can be made firm by insertion into the ground. The bottom row shows hurdles or short portable fences and these patterns can be used to make alcoves, arches, espaliers, and garden seats of corresponding character.

COPPICE WOOD FENCES, GATES, AND HURDLES.

Plate 51 *(Right)* A rustic gate under a rose-covered arch is a pretty addition to any country garden.

Plate 52 *(Below)* Furniture carved from tree roots, Ku Garden, Shanghai.

There was also a Greenhouse Aquarium and yet another Long Greenhouse, 100 feet in length, for wintering the plants used to ornament the gardens in summer.

The Ash Tent was a natural bower formed by the pendulous branches of weeping ash, and supported by pillars entwined with ivy; another feature known as 'The Rustic Orchestra' was able to seat 'His Grace's complete band' together with their stands for music'.[9] The Diamond Seat, protected by a magnificent elm, was a small rustic temple and took its name from the diamond panelling of the interior which was worked in the contrasting colours of birch, ash and hazel. This style of decoration, known as 'mosaic twig-work' became more and more popular in the Victorian age. It was used not only to enhance summerhouse interiors, but since it was suitable for use on any flat surface, it was also applied to furniture and to the exterior of buildings.

One of the easiest methods of applying mosaic twig-work to the interior of a garden building is to work the design onto panels. These can then be fixed to the internal walls of the building. For furniture, or the exterior of a building, it is better to apply the decoration after construction is complete.

First, the design must be marked out in pencil on the surface to be decorated. The thickest twigs, or slender branches of up to two inches in diameter, are most suitable for the exterior of a summerhouse, thinner rods for the internal decoration and the thinnest rods, of about half an inch in diameter, for fine decoration, and particularly for furniture.

After selecting straight rods of a uniform thickness these can be applied to the marked-out surface and secured with panel pins. Although beautiful patterns can be composed using twigs (usually hazel) of a similar thickness, a design may be varied by using slightly different thicknesses, and sticks of various colours.

The main lines of the design should be worked first, and for these one might use slightly thicker rods, or perhaps rods with a dark-coloured bark. The pattern can then be filled in with lighter-coloured sticks, such as peeled willow. Alternatively, slender pieces of silver birch could be used for the main lines, with a darker infill.

If the sticks are split through unequally, so that one half is a little less than a semicircle, they will fit together more tightly when pinned to the surface to be covered. When chunky designs are used on a summerhouse, it is fun to work odd-shaped pieces of timber into the design. A bole will make a grand rose for the centre of a summerhouse ceiling.

The Round Seat at Whiteknights was constructed with straight branches of maple and larch, beneath a circular thatched dome whose broad eaves gave shelter to a bench running round the interior. This bench extended through the wall, to form a semicircle on the outside rear of the building. This would be very simple to reconstruct in a garden today, as straight poles are readily available from garden centres and, if traditional thatch is not possible, shingles, or pine thatch (see Chapter 1) would make a suitable alternative.

Two conceits on a much grander scale were the Cedar Seat and another known simply as The Seat, which was the largest building at Whiteknights. The Cedar Seat was a fragrant bower and said to have been the most beautiful construction there, as well as curious in its interior construction. Even from a short distance away the materials are said to have seemed like a painting or embroidery. From this seat glimpses

The Round Seat, Whiteknights
'This seat is formed entirely of straight branches of the Maple and the Larch, beneath a circular
thatched dome: the rustic pillars support an architrave of taste and beauty, displayed in the most
simple materials. Thin slices from the heart of the Yew tree form medallions, which are grafted into
small sprays of the Larch tree with so much symmetry as to produce a surprising effect, and the
pebbled floor is disposed in leaves and circles with equal simplicity and grace'

of other conceits were caught between the trees and 'all is in unison with the sentiment
of retirement and calm seclusion suitable to the genius of the place'.[10]

The largest conceit, distinguished by its title, 'The Seat', combined elegance and
simplicity and was large enough to hold quite a party within. The flower-mantled
vista offered a view down Laburnum Bower, a tunnel of treillage some 1200 feet long.
There was also an Acacia Bower, 600 feet long, of rustic latticework entwined with
the branches of acacia trees, around which 'the pliant Woodbine wraps her tendrils,
loaded with flowers and shedding perfume'.[11] From here one could see the furze-
covered cottage in the distance, with little rustic seats on the way.

The 'Fishing Seat' was a rural bower, simply built from elm, which continued to
leaf, and with an interior of bark, thickly studded with moss. A walk through the
woodland brought one to the 'New Fishing Seat', also attractively built, from yew. Its
thatched roof was inlaid with rushes and finished with a thick surround of plaited rush.

Mrs Hofland wrote with literary affectation, but in a manner which aptly lent itself
to describing this wonderland of garden conceits. Unfortunately, however, the

splendour of Whiteknights was short-lived: George Spencer, the Marquis of Blandford, who succeeded in 1817 with a large inheritance as the 5th Duke of Marlborough was a notorious spendthrift. Blandford lavished money and attention on his garden throughout the war years, but eventually, thanks to his financial recklessness, all was doomed to a pitiful end. In 1804 he spent over £15,000 with the nursery of Messrs Lee and Kennedy, and he went on in this way until he fell into great financial difficulties. In spite of a loan of £50,000 in 1816, from Crasus Farquhar, a rich West Indian who had made a fortune from gunpowder, by 1817 he was in debt to the tune of £600,000, and his creditors finally forced the sale of Whiteknights, including the plants and garden structures. Mrs Hofland's work had indeed been a labour of love, since it is said that she was never paid for her painstaking and exquisite record.

The picturesque remained a popular style in rural areas and the rustic idiom steadily gathered momentum. The stimulation and curiosity aroused by the quaint qualities of a rustic scene caused the fashion for rustic ornament to spread from the celebrated gardens and picturesque estates and villages of the aristocracy to the gardens of the new suburban villas. Here, in the gardens of suburban 'boxes', the newly emerging middle class was keen to create a rustic scene to provide an idealized and rural atmosphere, and an escape from the toil and turmoil of industrial life.

The taste for rusticity was not confined to the British Isles, but spread as far afield as America, and later Australia. One man had a significant role to play in its world-wide popularity: John Claudius Loudon (1783–1843), a young Scot, was the first landscape designer of his time to focus attention on the suburban garden, and at the beginning of his career he announced himself as:

> ...the first who has set out as a landscape gardener, professing to follow Mr Price's principles. How far I shall succeed in executing my plans, and introducing more of the picturesque into improved places, time alone must determine.[12]

Loudon was to become the most influential landscape designer of his time, and his influence was to be widespread. Through his prolific writing of gardening books, and as founder and editor of *The Gardener's Magazine*, he encouraged landowners to provide decent cottages with gardens for their tenants, and subsequently compiled an encyclopaedia of cottage architecture.

Early in his career Loudon favoured an irregular garden design to complement the picturesque cottage, which he proposed should be part of the country estate or 'ferme ornée'. He approved of cottages in different national styles for ornamenting more extensive garden scenes. Swiss Cottages were already popular, and could be found on many estates around the British Isles and on the Continent. So, to the wide range of rustic garden buildings, the garden 'playrooms' of the eighteenth century, were now added these picturesque cottages, some of which had a more serious role to play, for Loudon recommended that they be used to house the upper servants of the house.

Although Loudon favoured permanent garden buildings of durable materials for those who could afford them, he did not reject the more simple kind. However, he did not approve of those that imitated the huts of primitive man. Wooden structures were introduced as protection from the weather, and ornamental rustic buildings were to be of artistic merit.

There is no limit to the wide variety of forms and patterns in which rustic features can be constructed by a person of ingenuity. So great was the impact of the rustic taste in Victorian times, that with the promotion of garden writers, and the great surge of garden books and new periodicals, it soon found popularity across the Atlantic.

In America, the young architect and landscape designer Andrew Jackson Downing (1815–1852), son of a nurseryman, became an ardent reader of British garden writers, particularly Loudon, by whom he was to be greatly influenced. However, feeling that Loudon's ideas were unsuitable for American soil, climate, and society, Downing set about adapting them to suit American conditions. He became the first important American author on landscape design and domestic architecture, publishing *A Treatise on the Theory and Practice of Landscape Gardening* (1841), and then *Cottage Residences* (1842). Downing hoped that one day the country residences of his homeland would rival the cottage homes of England, which were universally admired. A patriotic and religious man, Downing was keen to establish the American ideal that every man should own his own home. He advised that even the smallest home, with its garden, could be beautiful, and he proclaimed that usefulness was a necessary quality of that beauty. He believed that 'All BEAUTY is an outward expression of inward good'[13] and that care of the home – which acted as a barrier against vice, immorality and bad habits – was an important ingredient for making domestic life more delightful, binding family together, and strengthening patriotism. His influence was immeasurable and he could, perhaps, be said to be responsible for the development of the American picturesque suburbia found between tranquil countryside and harsh city.

Downing's landscape designs fell into two categories, 'the Beautiful', the polished landscape in accord with the grand and elegant mansions of the prosperous; and 'the Picturesque', more suited to the humble cottage or small villa. In 'the Beautiful', landscapes were gracefully curved with flowing lines expressing harmony and calm. Dignified groups of tall trees, with luxuriant branches, stood almost sweeping the turf of the gently undulating lawns; other graceful trees embellished the curved banks of smooth sheets of water. Easy winding brooks, crystal streams and firm, dry, clean gravel walks traversed the well-mown lawns. Within sight of the house were masses of flowering shrubs and everything was to be kept neat and orderly. Any rustic and picturesque elements, including rustic architecture and furniture, of which there was a great deal, were to be kept strictly out of sight of the house.

Downing's gardens followed the rules of the picturesque: Nature and Art displaying the same rude, violent, and irregular patterns. These were the qualities he felt were more suited to American conditions, its terrain, and the available materials. The rough timber of old and irregular trees, sudden variations of smooth and rough surfaces, secluded dells, wild cascades, and rugged rocks were all around and could be incorporated, or copied, at very little cost, and the maintenance cost too would be low.

Downing was considerate of the cottager's purse and asserted that beauty could be achieved by one perfectly grown tree in a mown lawn bordered by flowers and shrubs. He also proposed that, with a little ingenuity, rustic structures could be tastefully included in the picturesque scene.

Many of Downing's cottages were rich in rustic embellishment, particularly in the

Simple rustic porch at Canford Magna, Dorset

form of porches. Sometimes porches were added long after the house had been built and Downing suggested that to add a porch formed of cedar poles with the bark intact, would be far more becoming and less expensive than elaborate carpentry work. Porches give protection to an entrance and announce the identity of the owner, and porches of all kinds are still very popular. In the USA they tend to be large, often extend the length of the house, and are deep enough to become a living area. Rustic arbour porches are admired in Britain and, festooned with climbing plants, some stand firm and straight while others exploit the natural shape of knotted timber. Others may be decorated with fir cones or carved with flowers and rosettes. Twig mosaic too, is an interesting decoration for a porch. The porch is an ideal feature to cover with a drapery of leaf and blossom and a cottage with roses around the door is a traditional rural dream (Plates 18 and 19).

Downing also gave brief instructions for the construction of simple rustic buildings. One was for an unusual, covered rustic seat formed around a tree. To make the frame 12 posts are set firmly into the ground around the tree, and the openings between are filled in with irregular branches of different kinds of tree (rather like the porch on p. 72). The roof can be thatched, or made of board. A board roof might be decorated with a covering of bark, or slabs of tree with the bark left on.

After the erection of the Eiffel Tower in Paris (1889) there was a vogue for 'prospect towers'. In Australia, this novelty was taken up, regardless of the absence of a garden, but in America the prospect tower found a place in the garden. One, built near Brooklyn, was said to have been the first piece of rustic work of any size to have been constructed in America. If the spectator was raised some 20 or 30 feet above the ground, a new and exciting bird's-eye view could be very entertaining. Downing's design was for a rustic prospect tower of three storeys in height, with a spiral staircase winding round to the open-sided platforms of the second and upper storey, where there were seats under the double thatched roof.

Rustic porches, bridges, summerhouses and arbours all became popular in America but, tragically, Andrew Jackson Downing lost his life in a steamboat disaster in 1852, when only 37 years old. However, he is remembered not only for the picturesque suburbs of north-eastern America, but also by his success (inspired by Loudon) in merging English styles with the American landscape.

With the help of his assistant, Calvert Vaux, a Frenchman Downing had met when visiting England in 1850, Downing laid out the grounds around the White House and the New Smithsonian Institute, both in Washington D.C. They were also keen to promote the public park, and Vaux went to work with Frederick Law Olmstead (1822–1903) in laying out Central Park, New York. The city authorities had realized that New York was becoming so congested with buildings and traffic, that if they did not act quickly all the open spaces would disappear. A competition was held for the design of Central Park and from 32 entrants the design of Frederick Law Olmstead and Calvert Vaux was chosen.

Rustic porch at Canford Magna, with an unusual flat roof where rustic urns once stood. Built by local thatcher, John Hicks, c.1898

Rustic porch at Shepton Mallet

The look-out, One Tree Hill, Fern Tree Gully, Victoria, c.1900

It was a rugged site that varied considerably in levels and so, of course, readily lent itself to the picturesque. The aim of the designers was to develop a number of rural scenes within the rocky, wooded hillside and the contrasting broad slopes higher up, and to achieve this plan a system of sunken roads was laid, so as to keep the park clear of traffic. There were, of course, situated within the pockets of pictursque beauty, many rustic features.

It was this chain of events that shows how the ideas of Loudon and Downing were carried forward into the parks of the USA. Traditional-style rustic buildings were frequently built in city parks, but occasionally a more bizarre design would appear, like the 'Spruce Log', Palmer Park, Detroit, Michigan. Palmer Park was built on land donated to the city by ex-Senator Thomas W. Palmer, in 1893, and became one of the city's favourite breathing spaces. The Spruce Log Cabin, at the centre of the park, was an exact reproduction of the home in which Senator Palmer had lived when Detroit was little more than a trading post.

In Australia, the homes of the early pioneer settlers were, of necessity, built in a rustic style; a style which in other parts of the world was considered ornamental. The

Shaded seats for Central Park, New York. Calvert Vaux, 1874

settler had to be innovative, and make use of materials with which he was quite unfamiliar. Homesteads, farmyards, and outhouses were constructed with whatever materials came to hand, and this was usually timber. A homestead may have been simply a hut built of logs and bark with a chimney of twigs and mud. When clearing the land of tree roots it was found that the bulbous mallee root (one of the many species of the eucalypt) was so tough that it could be used as a substitute for stone. The roots were fitted together and bound with mud to build walls. The earliest roofs were constructed with bark, usually the stringy bark from the box tree. The bark was stripped from the trunk in sheets of about 6 feet by 3 feet, fastened to the roof by

*Spruce Log, Palmer Park,
Detroit, a log cabin that
first belonged to Senator
Palmer*

means of a wooden frame, and held down by rawhide straps. Other roofs were formed with mallee branches, and thatched with reed, cereal straw, or even wiry grass. Alternatively, shingles were sometimes used to cover these strong buildings.

The interiors of these primitive dwellings were lined with boards, and sometimes lathed and plastered for greater comfort. The ceilings of some of them were lined with sailcloth stretched tightly across the timber frames; this was used to exclude the draughts that occurred when the timbers shrank due to seasoning. In the Bear's Hut at Killerton, Devon, the ceiling of the 'hermit's chapel' is lined with hide, and in the main room straw matting decorated with pine-cones makes an attractive alternative. These are two ideas possibly adapted from methods used in genuine primitive dwellings.

The typical homestead was planted with exotic pines among casuarinas and eucalypts, to provide shade-giving windbreaks. There would have been an orchard producing apples, apricots, and figs, so it was essential to build a fruit room. This would have been a half cellar giving protection from the fierce summer heat, where fruit and other perishable foods could be stored in a cool atmosphere. A pit was dug and the walls retained by timber. A shingled roof, left open at each end, would be pitched across it to form what was perhaps the coolest place on the settlement. This ancient method is similar to the way that ice-houses were constructed in the landscape gardens of Europe and North America.

Ornamental rustic buildings were built in Australia, but it was several decades later that the vogue for the picturesque eventually found its way to this part of the world. Until the 1820s, Australian interest in architecture and garden design was largely confined to timber buildings for necessary shelter, and gardens for growing essential fruit and vegetables. When thought was given to flowers, it was usually a reminder of home. Roses and climbers clothed the verandahs and popular flowers for the 'picking gardens' were roses, pinks, and stocks. However, it was the iris, geranium, yucca,

Gold digger's hut showing roof of large plates of bark. Victoria, 1905

argave, oleander, and bamboo that would eventually win the hearts of the gardeners, as these plants are more tolerant of the Australian climate.

By the 1820s the pioneers had established their roots, and increased prosperity and leisure time made way for more interest in garden design. In spite of irregular rainfall and regular heat, which were not ideal conditions, it was the style of the English landscape parks of Capability Brown and Humphry Repton that were taken as the models Australians set out to follow.

Thomas Shepherd (d.1834), a nurseryman from Hackney, England, and previously trained by a student of Brown, emigrated to New South Wales and attempted to educate the Australian public by giving a series of lectures in Sydney on horticulture and landscape. The lectures were later published as the first books on gardening related to Australian conditions and concerned with converting the natural bush into landscape scenery. It is uncertain how much influence Shepherd had, but it was a combination of the landscape and the picturesque movements which were to become popular in the fashionable residential quarter to the east of Sydney, more specifically, the gardens at Elizabeth Bay (1835). Nevertheless, this was many decades after the picturesque had made its mark in England. The picturesque required a variety of garden ornaments and architectural features, and having had so much experience in the use of timber for their early homes, Australians were competent to build attractive garden buildings. Rustic bridges, summerhouses, and gazebos intermingled with castellated ruins, and half-timbered cottages punctuated parklands.

When the Victorian taste for ornamentation began to exert itself, the Gardenesque[14] extended to the plants themselves, and massed colours and textures of carpet bedding became of the utmost importance; however, the taste for rustic garden buildings remained.

Rustic iron bridge, Rippon Lea, Melbourne

Rippon Lea, Melbourne, is said to be the finest surviving late nineteenth-century High Victorian garden around an Australian suburban property. A gravel drive, overhung by Moreton Bay Figs, winds its way to the *porte cochère* of the mansion of polychrome brickwork. Wide lawns, fringed with deciduous oaks, elms, and evergreen conifers, sweep down from the house to an extensive lake, fed by a stream appearing from the magnificent fern house. The lake is punctuated by islands linked by rustic cast-iron bridges which echo the ornamental rustic theme of the variously-sized summerhouses, and there are benches of bark-covered branches.

By the 1870s there was a fashion for families to retreat to the mountains to avoid the summer heat. At first, timber cottages were erected, which were later converted and enlarged to become quite substantial houses. In the gardens were lakes and follies, and shingled pavilions were built amongst the exotic plantations of camellias, azaleas and rhododendrons. The Australian style of garden design began to exert itself, and the picturesque scene was absorbed into the gardens whilst pretty garden houses gave shelter from the summer sun.

The gardens of the earlier homesteads of the pioneers have now become well established. Trees planted a century ago are now mature, and the fussy Victorian gardens have given way to broad sweeping lawns. Some homesteads of previous decades are now sought after as toy houses, to be admired as rustic follies.

5

THE VICTORIAN RUSTIC GARDEN

The rage for rustic gardens enjoyed its heyday in Victorian England. So popular was the rustic style that cartoons featuring rustic work frequently appeared in *Punch* and the first ever Christmas card, printed in 1843, showed a festive family-party scene framed by swirling branches and vines in true rustic fashion.[1] However, although this card marked the beginning of a long tradition of the exchange of Christmas greetings, there was some protest by do-gooders of the day, who felt that a picture of people drinking would encourage drunkenness!

In spite of the Victorian reputation for being staid, Victorians did know how to enjoy themselves, and the 'country seat' continued to be a venue for fun and entertainment. Hunting and shooting have always been popular country-house sports, and at that time many estates bred or kept their own pack of hounds, often housed in smart purpose-built kennels in the estate park. At one time stag-hunting took precedence, but, after the Duke of Beaufort introduced fox-hunting at Badminton in 1782 the latter became an almost compulsory pursuit to be enjoyed by the landed gentry.

However, deer stalking continued to be popular in Scotland, where Prince Albert was a frequent and keen participant, and at least one of the rustic lodges built in the landscape park around Taymouth Castle, which Prince Albert is known to have visited with Queen Victoria in 1842, has now become a monument to the sport.

Taymouth Castle, Kenmore, was rebuilt and remodelled several times on an extremely lavish and luxurious scale, and in 1752 the 3rd Earl of Breadlebane built several follies and lodges around the park. In contrast to the stark architecture of the castle, the keepers' lodges were later embellished with porches supported by solid tree trunks, and richly decorated with rustic-work.

Fort Lodge, on the south-east side of the park is perhaps unique in its decoration. The undulating eaves of the slate roof are supported by trunks of pine, painted bright red, which form a canopy. This canopy shelters a row of three stags' heads below, which thrust boldly through sunbursts of silver-birch branches, which they wear like baronial haloes. Regally poised, the display of these 'Monarchs of the Glen' may have been inspired by one of Sir Edwin Landseer's (1802–1873) many paintings of this noble animal that came to play such an important part in Victorian imagery. Landseer was thrilled by his first visit to Scotland in 1824, and was quick to move in high society and to take part in deer-stalking expeditions.

The craftsmanship of the rustic-work in Fort Lodge is superb. The straight branches of birch have been carefully cut into lengths that taper to the central point of the sunburst, and they have, of course, been allowed to keep their beautiful silver bark.

Darker pieces of branch mark out a cross within the sunburst pattern, and these darker-coloured branches curve at the perimeter to form a frame enclosing each sunburst design. This pattern, minus the stags' heads, is repeated on the side door of Rustic Cottage, on the other side of the park, but, generally, the rustic-work here is more intricate and less startling. Again, the eaves of this one-storey cottage are supported by red-painted columns of pine trunks, which form a porch with deliciously decorated vaulting. The ceiling, constructed with pine boards, is embellished with a pattern of twig diamonds, about 12 inches across, each decorated at the centre with a polished medallion formed by cutting a slice from across a branch of about three inches in diameter (Plate 19).

Many buildings in this area have porches supported by pine trunks and many may have been once decorated with rustic-work. There are presently one or two cottages being refurbished, but unfortunately it looks unlikely that the rustic-work will be restored.

The parkland, where Queen Victoria and Prince Albert once enjoyed a grand fête with bagpipes, dancing, and fireworks, is now a golf course and several local follies remain in the area. Rustic buildings continued to be popular and many a great house had a rustic retreat in the garden for use as a tea-house or a children's playroom. Some rustic huts were used to house strange guests, and the rustic cottage at Killerton, Devon (one of the properties of the Acland family, bequeathed to the National Trust, and still a great attraction) has given shelter to some unusual characters.

The gardens at Killerton are spectacular in the spring, when the blossom of azaleas, rhododendrons and camellias brings the whole garden to life. It was originally laid out by the young Scotsman John Veitch, who came to 'lay out a park' and then went on, with the help of Sir Thomas Acland, to found the great empire of Veitch nurseries, which extended to London, and continued to be famous in Exeter until the 1960s.[2]

Sir Thomas Acland brought his new wife Lydia home to Killerton, in 1808 and soon after had a pretty rustic cottage built for her, which she called Lady Cott. This pretty building is a pastoral gem, decorated inside and out in the most minute rustic

The first Christmas card, 1843.
The rustic taste spread to
Christmas cards and cartoons in
Punch

Under the canopy of the porch at Fort Lodge, Kenmore, are a row of three stags' heads thrusting through sunbursts of silver birch. The columns supporting the porch are painted bright red

detail, with materials collected from the surrounding countryside. It is built with straight poles of pine arranged vertically, and relieved with a herringbone pattern each side of a latticed bay window. The timbers beneath the deep and heavy thatch of the gable are decorated with pine-cones.

A door, composed of criss-cross branches, opens on to a small entrance hall, where the walls and ceiling are lined with woven-willow panels and the floor is cobbled with pebbles set in a diamond pattern. In the main room, the theme of woven willow continues in a basketwork seat built into an alcove clad with the same material. The walls of this room are lined with rush matting, as is the ceiling, which is also decorated with pine-cones pinned into geometric patterns. A quaint feature is an additional round window above a bay, which penetrates the deep wall in a similar way to the 'wind eyes' of early mud hovels, which were formed by penetrating the thick wall with half of an open-ended barrrel.[3] A pattern of sawn logs radiates from the centre of the floor to the fireplace and the shelves where, no doubt, the tea cups were once stored.

Entrance to the third room, known as 'The Hermit's Chamber' (although there is no record of a hermit having lived here) is through a half-door veneered with bark. A gothic window, made of irregular pieces of stained glass, throws light upon a floor patterned in diamonds of deer's knuckle-bones; the ceiling has a covering of animal hide. An imposing looking rustic throne is tucked into an alcove at the side of the window. The deep windowsill is like an altar in this tiny sanctuary where once the gardener might, now and again, have enjoyed a quiet pipe, however, such occasions would have been rare, for Lord Acland often took tea here.

The hut was built on the same level as the children's nursery on the first floor of the big house, so they always had easy access and tea things and kindling for the fire were always kept ready. Lady Lydia Acland had 10 children and 37 grandchildren, so there must have been numerous tea-parties until the hut became the home of a bear, brought home from Canada by Sir Thomas's son Gilbert! From this time on the cottage has been known as The Bear's Hut, but this was not the last of the unusual guests given shelter there. During the Second World War the big house was used by a couple of schools evacuated from Kent, one a boys' school and the other a girls' school. Consequently, space was at such a high premium that some staff were glad to find themselves sleeping in the Bear's Hut!

Not far away, in Bicton Park, near Exmouth, is a summerhouse built on the edge of the pinetum and overlooking a lake. It is an octagonal building, built with fish-scale shingles, and sturdy tree trunks supporting the gables of the wings on each side. It is called 'The Hermitage', although no hermit is known to have lived there. It was built by the head gardener of Bicton Park, Robert Glendenning, for Lady Louisa Rolle in 1839. The date is expertly marked out in mosaic twigwork below the eaves, along with various symbols and patterns. The large, thick shingles of the two-tier pyramid roof are unusually decorated with carved rosettes. In spite of the decay that is now taking over the little building, it is perhaps the most supreme example of its kind. The interior too, is superb. The ceiling is lined with basketwork, and the light from the coloured glazing in the windows casts a warm glow over the floor, which is paved with the knucklebones of Bicton deer (see p. 159 and Plate 20).

During the Victorian era the gardening middle class started to reap the full benefit of improved printing techniques, and when Shirley Hibberd (1825–1890), writer and

Rustic reading-room-cum-bee-shed, c.1870

great favourite of the Victorians, published *Rustic Adornments for Homes of Taste* (1856) it was a huge success and rapidly went into three editions. (It was perhaps a compliment that it was pirated by Edward Sprague Read for a series of his own books in the USA.)

Shirley Hibberd, like Downing (p. 68), was anxious to focus on the home. With social improvement now concentrated on housing, he felt it was time to extend this trend to the appreciation of beauty and promotion of moral refinement in the home. His contribution was to promote the idea of the superiority of Art over Nature. He published a collection of hobbies of the rustic kind, to embellish *Homes of Taste*, that would benefit country folk and town dwellers alike. In true Victorian style, he embraced patriotism, morality, and religious attitudes, feeling that they too could be improved by his ideas.

The summerhouse was the most important feature of the Victorian rustic garden. What greater pleasure than to spend a peaceful hour enjoying 'book and bottle' in the quiet seclusion of a summerhouse, accompanied only by bird song, and the sweet fragrance of flowers wafting across on a summer breeze as it gently rustles the bamboo. However, Hibberd had other ideas: first the summerhouse had to be built! There was advice for suburban gardeners on construction and care of rustic features, which may have been the first published DIY text! Enterprisingly, Hibberd gave instructions for making a temporary DIY summerhouse, a seven-sided affair of wire-netting frames, bolted together and planted around with an abundance of quick-growing climbers. Annuals, he suggested, were preferable, but clematis and everlasting pea would also be suitable, as they may be cut down in autumn when the summerhouse should be dismantled. (Mr Hibberd was obviously undisturbed by the story of the sweet retreat for spiders, straggled with honeysuckles and jessamine, the venue of the well-known scene between Mr Tracy Tupman and Miss Wardle in *Pickwick Papers*!)

By the 1900s Mr Hibberd's dream had come true, and Coopers, of the Old Kent Road, in London, were able to supply a prefabricated 'Thatched Roof Summerhouse, No. 305, enclosed with door and windows of cathedral glass, handsomely fitted throughout...' all for £32. Summerhouses ranged in size from very small to very large, containing two or more rooms. They were hidden behind a variety of façades, from formal Grecian or Victorian Gothic of stone, to more homespun rustic buildings, constructed using the crooked limbs of trees.

To satisfy the practical-minded Victorians, garden buildings became less frivolous, and were more usually built to serve a utilitarian purpose, as well as providing pleasant retreats. Above all, the summerhouse had to look as though it was used, or it would lose its ornamental effect: a home for bees or birds, a tool shed or fruit room, or even a display of curiosities; as now, most people enjoyed collecting something. Today there is seldom room to spare in the house and another member of the family might complain about a collection of oddities: china, clay pipes, shells, or even a hoard of old straw hats. However, arranged in a summerhouse, such a collection could take on a new dimension.

Traditionally, summerhouses should be clothed with greenery, an especially good idea if the building is run down and ugly. However, if it is a pretty building, it is better to carefully choose a few climbers which will mingle harmoniously to enhance the building rather than smother it. As the summerhouse is designed as a place in which to loiter, it offers a splendid opportunity to grow a selection of fragrant plants and shrubs chosen for flowering in both winter and summer.

Every old gardening book gives advice on beekeeping, once an important part of country living. Honey was an essential ingredient of mead, and the staple sweetener before sugar was widely available. By Victorian times, honey was no longer regarded as a necessity, but more of a luxury, so beekeeping ceased to be strictly for country folk, and many town dwellers realized that this hobby could bring a touch of country life into their back gardens. Today this trend continues, and many people living in towns enjoy keeping bees, and take pride in planting their gardens with their bees' favourite flowers.

The kitchen garden, by tradition, is the place for beehives, but standing the hives in a rustic beehouse can make an attractive feature in a flower garden, as long as it is distanced from busy garden paths and walks.

Housing for bees has become more and more elaborate through the ages. Once it consisted of a slate ledge on the side of a house, on which the straw bee-skeps stood. Then came bee-boles, the niches for skeps to sit in, built into a wall, and later came the more ornate bee-sheds, or honey-houses as they are sometimes known, which formed part of the picturesque scene, as did the fancy dairies or pigsties of the 'fermes ornées'.

Although useful, bee-houses are not a necessity in temperate climates (such as the British Isles) but in countries that have extremes of temperature, shelter is important. A light frost will not harm bees if they have plenty to eat, but bees thrive best if their hives are sheltered from the direct rays of the sun. Honey-houses should be kept cool in summer, and good ventilation is the best cooling system. Honey-houses can be useful for the storage of combs, as a workshop for equipment repair and manufacture during off-season, and, in Canada, they are sometimes used to protect both the bees and their honey against bears!

The straw skep, formed from wreaths of straw, is still made, and, being lightweight and flexible, is very useful if collecting swarms from inaccessible corners. The skep made of mud and straw is also attractive, and a skep left standing in a summerhouse makes a pretty conversation piece in a rustic garden.

The ideal Victorian bee-shed was one with a hipped roof of timber, supported on strong uprights of larch, with its bark left on for picturesque effect, and, over the timber roof, a layer of felt that had been well pitched and dusted with sand. As seen in the engraving of the Apiary in Shirley Hibberd's garden at Stoke Newington, it can be open on all sides, but in winter months it should be roughly boarded up, leaving just a small opening for bees to go in and out.

There are many natural sources of pollen in the British Isles, although it can be scarce early in the year, but in Australia and the USA the beekeeper should be wary of seasonal shortages, for lack of pollen can cause the extinction of a bee colony. When bees begin to stir after the long winter months they are quite drowsy, and incapable of long flights. A host of spring pollen-bearing flowers grown fairly near to their hives is very convenient for the bees. The flowers of bulbous plants are especially welcome in the spring garden, and there are many of these whose pollen is enjoyed by bees.

A very small summerhouse can be constructed with the front made in an open design, thus allowing a pleasant view and giving the occupant a feeling of spaciousness. Small, 'Punch-and-Judy'-sized summerhouses of this style were frequently offered for sale in Victorian times by suburban woodyards. The fronts were formed with branches, whilst the back and sides were of finished wood.

When constructing a summerhouse of this size, it is important to leave adequate ventilation between the roof and the sides, to ensure an adequate circulation of air to keep the temperature low. An attractive timber for the front posts is yew, the supporting posts could be larch poles (available from most garden centres), and the lattice-work hazel rods. Fruit wood too, from trees pruned in autumn, is useful for decoration.

If the inside of the summerhouse is to be decorated, it can be lined with plywood to give a good base for any decorative panels of twig mosaic. The roof can have a covering of roofing felt or, for a more picturesque effect, a thatch of reed, straw, or heather. The floor can be of pebble paving, stone, modern composition slabs, or sawn logs on end, set into the soil. These can easily be replaced if they should rot. However, if a floor of wooden boards is chosen, a plastic sheet, such as that used for lining a pond, prevents damp rising. The ends of supporting posts benefit from being given a good coat of bitumen as a precaution against dampness. Another precaution is to have the summerhouse bolted to a raised concrete or stone kerb.

The moss-house was an alternative to the summerhouse and its decoration was a favourite hobby of Victorian ladies. There is a great variety of mosses around the countryside worldwide, but although grown in Japan, in special Moss Gardens, these

Straw bee-skep

Shirley Hibberd's apiary at Stoke Newington, c.1870

are seldom found cultivated in other parts of the world. In Western countries, rather than appreciate the exquisite structure of moss, we spend a great deal of time eradicating it from our lawns. However, whilst Victorian gentlemen were kept busy making summerhouses or keeping bees, ladies in America and Britain collected moss, or bought it specially from their nurserymen, to decorate both the inside and the outside of moss-houses, fashioned to resemble a multi-coloured tapestry.

The common tree moss, or more correctly, lichen, was a favourite for moss-houses, so too was *Cenomyce rangiferina*, or the white Reindeer Moss, found frequently on ash trees, or on gravelly heathlands. It was recommended that mosses be dried to retain 'almost their full colour and perfectness'[4] and this was done by laying them upper side down upon the earth in a dark cellar until perfectly dry. For even better colour, mosses could be dyed; feather moss was said to be the prettiest for this: after removing dirt and sticks, the easiest method was to use 'family dyes' of 'bottle green and leather colours'.[5]

To make a moss-house, the skeleton, or framework, of the house or arbour is formed and small rods (about half an inch in diameter) are nailed over the whole surface to form a rustic lathing. Small quantities of wood-moss of different colours are collected and, taking small pieces in the hand, the roots are thrust closely together between the rods using a small wooden wedge. The tufted ends are then spread out

(Opposite:) Clay bee-skep

'Punch and Judy Summerhouse', c.1870

to cover the rods, leaving a smooth surface of mosses of different colours. If the colours are carefully chosen and equally carefully arranged, it is said to have an effect not unlike that of a thick Brussels carpet. The mosses retain their colour for a considerable length of time, and when properly rammed in with a wedge they cannot be pulled out again without breaking their tops.

There must once have been a 'moss-mania', for one quaint Victorian craft book gives instructions for making many moss items. A 'Moss Hat' could be quite a joke hanging among a collection of straw hats in the summerhouse, even if you did not fancy wearing it.

> To Make A Moss Hat:
> Take a man's old straw hat and rip three or four rows of braid from it, then fasten the ends on firm, and make a handle of it. Put pasteboard in the inside of the crown, then line it with white paper, and cover it with moss.[6]

Another remarkable feature of Victorian Gardens was the 'stumpery' or 'rootery', planted with those so much admired ferns. The remains of a stumpery still sustains a bank in the beautiful gardens of Biddulph Grange, Staffordshire, created in the mid-eighteenth century and greatly admired in Victorian times. Biddulph was owned by James Bateman, a man well-known for his achievements in the gardening world and, with the help of Edward W. Cooke, Biddulph underwent rapid transformation, was opened to the public, talked about, written about, and soon became very influential, its garden features being copied from Keswick to Crystal Palace Park. It is believed that E. W. Cooke may have been responsible for the stumpery, or rootery, as they were sometimes called, at Crystal Palace, as well as the one at Biddulph.

The use of roots in gardens had been recognized as a Chinese device for over a century. It is, therefore, appropriate that at Biddulph roots and stumps jut out from the banks at the side of a path leading to a cavernous passage to that part of the garden known as 'China'. Here, there is a Chinese pavilion overlooking a pool, and nearby a little tea-house with a ceiling decorated with a mosaic of rustic twig-work.

The stumpery is an ideal place for ferns and woodland plants to grow among rugged, weathered tree stumps and the contorted trunks of aged, pollarded, or deformed oaks and roots. With the addition of bold pieces of rockwork protruding here and there, they look as though they are a natural outcrop from the ground or bank. Cavities become nests for ferns, and trailing or woodland plants, and protuberances give support to climbers. Created in the partial shade of trees, the stumpery provides an environment wholly suited to ferns, in which their roots are kept cool, but where other plants may prove difficult to rear. Suited to any space where it catches a variety of sunshine and shadow, it can even be situated on the north-facing side of a garden, if that provides varied positions and aspects. If there is a cascade of water, tumbling over some rocks and collecting mosses on its way, this adds still further to the attraction.

Sawn log floor for a summerhouse

The most interesting gardens are those which are full of surprises and secret places; a stumpery, approached through a rustic arch constructed from weathered roots held together with wooden pegs and clothed with climbers, makes an intriguing feature. A shady dell near the summerhouse would be a good spot, or, the stumpery could be the perfect feature to form a screen and to hide the summerhouse from view.

When building a stumpery, you must take into account the materials available in your part of the town or country. In towns it can be difficult to find stumps or tree butts (however, the local parks department are often pleased to get rid of such things). As for construction, dig out a broad, irregular trench and throw up the earth to form banks and knolls, which can be faced with brick 'burrs', or 'bats' (these are the odd pieces of brick from the kiln that have been spoilt in the firing process). To make the feature more picturesque, add large weathered tree roots – including the stool, or base of the tree after the trunk has been cut down to the ground – placed in a haphazard fashion, with rocks piled here and there. Cavities should be filled with sandy peat to form nests for plants, and the banks and knolls need a coating of the same mixture, varying in depth from six to eighteen inches. A rock removed here and there gives extra depth and allows roots to penetrate well into the ground. Provision must be made for displaying larger plants boldly, while at the same time providing nooks and crannies for tinier plants; plants can then be grown in positions suitable to their variety. No collection of rocks, stumps, or roots should ever begin or end abruptly, but should merge gradually with the adjoining ground, by means of a few, carelessly scattered roots, and/or small rocks, to get a natural effect (Plate 26).

An alternative to a large stumpery could be two or three large roots or butts of trees grouped together on the lawn with mould and plants placed in their interstices. Roots, stumps, and rocks should be arranged carefully and deliberately, or the feature may look like an old heap that has been left behind on the lawn, rather than an ornamental feature.

Whether as fountain, cascade, pond, or trickling stream, water is one of the most attractive elements in a garden. It can instantly create a variety of moods: still water, with its mysterious, shadowy reflections of trees and clouds gently gliding beneath the surface brings calm and serenity; a stream gurgling over pebbles animates the scene, bringing life and movement. In summer, the water may sparkle and the air feel refreshingly cooler at its sight, or the haze of the early morning mist may merge water and cloud to hide a secret place within their midst. In winter, ice or snow, or a hoar frost on the trees around the bank can transform the scene to a glistening winter wonderland.

Clever use of water can make a garden seem much larger, but remember that a stream should never appear to spring out of the bare ground. Even if only a few yards long, it should seem to flow into the garden from somewhere far beyond, to give a feeling of space.

At Cliveden, Buckinghamshire, there is a rustic bridge at the edge of the lake in the Chinese garden. This pretty bridge, which borrows its design from the Chinese style, is carefully constructed with a hand-rail of yew whose natural curves are used to their best advantage. It is a clever device, giving the impression that from under its arch a river flows in and broadens into the lake. This is not so, the pretty rustic bridge is on the edge of the lake. This bridge has a practical purpose as well as an

*The Yukon Bridge.
Length: 22 foot; width:
6 foot*

aesthetic one, and that is to disguise machinery that lies beneath. If the bridge is crossed over and passed by on the path below, one realizes that the bridge is, in fact, at the edge of the lake and the machinery remains hidden from view by a mass of large leaves.

In a small garden, a bridge should be of a quiet and simple character: just a rough plank with bark left on the edges could be enough, with a hand-rail for safety if the water is deep. A larger bridge needs a foundation. This can be made by laying down a few large square paving stones beneath the surface, on both sides of the stream; upon these are stretched two round posts with the bark on, of about eight inches in diameter, or alternatively, a pair of sleepers. The floor of the bridge is made by laying small posts of equal size, about six inches in diameter, crosswise upon the sleepers and securely nailing them down. Bark can be left intact on all the wood used, and if a more ornamental bridge is required a panel or two of twig and cone-work can be incorporated, or pieces of root fastened on with wire in an attractive arrangement. The simple rustic bridge above has been designed by Richard and Janet Strombeck. It is plain and substantial and would look well in a variety of gardens.

No rustic bridge should be left bare; a suitable selection of plants, trees, or shrubs should be planted nearby, at the water's edge. The willow is a traditional tree in both the English and American landscape, and a landscape with water seems incomplete without some sort of willow growing nearby. There are about 500 species of willow in all, and the weeping willow, *Salix babylonica*, is perhaps the grandest of them all. It is extremely easy to grow: just push a twig or slim branch into damp soil and in no time at all you will have a new tree. The graceful greenery, gently brushing the water, provides the perfect place for ducks to dart and dive among the trailing branches. However, the willow needs space, since a mature tree can reach 25 feet and a large willow by a tiny stream looks absurd. *Salix matsudana* 'Tortuosa' could be an alternative; its attraction is in its contorted structure; every branch and twig is curled, almost corkscrew fashion. It has an upright habit and, because it is slow-growing, it is easy to keep trimmed down, to maintain a compact specimen tree which could stand beside water even in a small garden.

Last, but not least, are the smaller features of the Victorian rustic garden. Log edging for flowerbeds is now available by the metre, rustic tripods can be used as

Tree stumps and butts for the stumpery, arriving at the RHS Chelsea Flower Show, 1989

frames for climbing plants, and rustic poles and rope swags of roses never fail to please. Rustic flower-stands, baskets, and vases used as an alternative to classical vases or urns are a feature that have not, alas, continued to find a place in our gardens, although they were once used to bring studs of colour to the lawns of many celebrated houses.

These containers can be made in a variety of shapes and sizes: a tripod of branches of trees might form a pedestal, if one is required, and an octagonal box shape could form the body. Mosaic twig-work can be used to decorate the box. Alternatively, the outside can be encased with pieces of fir wood or old larch wood with the bark left on, and decorated with festoons of cones. The interior of the container can be coated with bitumastic paint, and then with a lining of plastic stapled to the inside to prevent oil from the bitumen getting into the soil. Holes should also be made in the base of the box shape for drainage.

In days gone by, these containers were used for showy flowers: brightly coloured nasturtiums, pelargoniums, ferns, and fuchsias, and the new exotics finding their way across the world.

As winner of the *Sunday Times* 'Design a period garden' competition, the author's Victorian Rustic Garden was built and exhibited at the Royal Horticultural Society

Chelsea Flower Show (1989) from a design using the ideas and features described in this chapter. The site allocated was unexpectedly sloping, so Victorian tiles were used to decorate the surface of a raised viewing platform, which helped to make the ground level. Unfortunately, this had to cut into the garden space allowed (which was 40 feet × 60 feet) so only two-thirds of the whole design was built. The fence surrounding the garden was made from larch poles arranged in a simple pattern, and the garden was entered by a rustic gate made from knotty branches with a bole to form a focal point in the design (Plates 21 to 27).

The original plan for the garden was made up of two circular areas: the area closest to the (imaginary) house was cut down to a semicircle, and gravelled to provide an area for menial tasts; overall a country-cottage style prevailed. It was here that the rustic-covered pump stood by the stream separating the two halves of the garden, and if there had been a white cottage wall hollyhocks would have straggled in front of it, and nicotiana would have scented the evening air, rather like the picturesque cottage at Old Warden (Plate 15).

The rough gravel was softened by a series of rustic tripods covered with ivy, roses, and clematis to retain interest all year round. Three circular beds of roses, underplanted with culinary herbs, were balanced by three lavender bushes also planted in the gravel. Small plants at the front of the herbaceous borders were allowed to creep into the gravel to soften the edges.

The little stream appeared to flow from beneath a mound of stone and then out to the edge of the garden. One bank was lined with wattle in traditional style (colour plate 6), the other was retained by logs of silver birch. The stream was crossed by a bridge of larch poles and silvery birch timbers. The larch hand-rails of the bridge were patterned at the centre with spiral markings, making them more picturesque. British television personality Alan Titchmarsh commented that spiral patterns of this sort are made by honeysuckle twisting and turning its way up young trees as they grow. In his 'neck of the wood', which is Hampshire, he told us that such trees are known as 'witch sticks', and are meant to repel all kinds of evil spirits.

The golden gravel was carried over the surface of the bridge to continue as a path curving around the circular lawn, thus uniting the two halves of the garden. This path passed a shrubbery on the eastern side of the garden, and was flanked on the edge closest to the lawn by a colonnade of larch pillars, linked by swags of thick cable rope draped with roses. The path led on to the summerhouse, bedecked with fragrant climbers. This little building, thatched with reed, was attractively lined with rustic-work, and had a floor of sawn logs. Blue and red glass, Victorian style, was included in the twig mosaic that lined the interior, and there was a pattern of cones and teazles on the ceiling. The furniture in the summerhouse was very simple, just a triangular table and a couple of benches. However, I also designed the more complicated, rustic lovers' seat, and this was made by Mr Amos of Wye, Kent.

The view from the summerhouse was towards the stumpery, or fernery, that spread across the opposite corner. This caused a great deal of comment because a stumpery is such an unusual feature these days. The tree butts arrived on a huge open truck and it was a tricky business choosing which ones would look well together once they were off the truck and in the garden. However, that evening, I stayed behind with L. John Bailey, who had no end of patience in arranging and rearranging the heavy pieces

One of the rustic bridges built of iron, Rippon Lea, Melbourne

Buttes Chaumont Park, Paris, was created on the site of a series of enormous old quarries said to have been originally surrounded by acres of rubbish. By cutting away the ground on three sides of the quarries, and leaving the highest and most picturesque side intact, a new park was landscaped. The open lawns with tasteful fringes of shrubs and groups of trees still exist and masses of rocks form peaks and valleys. There is an enormous stalactite cave 60 feet in height from floor to ceiling, and an imposing cliff rising to a height of over 160 feet and semicircled by an artificial lake. What were once carriage drives around the park remain linked by footpaths that meander their way, sometimes cut into steps, across the valleys, around the peaks, and over the bridges. One bridge is a suspension bridge, more than 200 feet long. The lake is supplied by two rivulets which run through two valleys of the park; one of these cascades into a cavern over 100 feet deep.[2] Strong fences were needed for safety, and what better than reinforced concrete, made to look like timber rustic-work, and suitably in keeping with the nearby restaurants, built like Swiss chalets in the picturesque style.

(Opposite:) The Indian Kiosk, The Swiss Garden, Old Warden

Buttes Chaumont is still a popular park and the fences are still in good condition; however, obviously well cared for, they do look rather pristine compared with a beautiful rustic bridge of reinforced concrete at the Parc Botanique de la Fosse, in the Loire valley. This bridge has aged beautifully, the concrete developing a patina of green moss, giving it a soft natural appearance, which blends with the landscape. The Arboretum de la Fosse (within the Parc Botanique), covering some 60 acres of hills, has been planted over several generations with a magnificent collection of trees, plants, and shrubs as they have been discovered around the world. Carefully designed paths and clearings are bordered with plants, which are interesting both from a scientific and an aesthetic point of view. *Cyclamen neapolitanum* fill the glades and *Nerine bowdenii* grows along the walls leading to the lawn. The site had no natural water supply, but a rivulet was fed from a large reservoir, principally to irrigate the park. This reservoir is regularly replenished by four hydraulic rams situated on a stream in the Loire valley 60 metres lower in altitude and at a distance of 1800 metres. The little bridge, constructed in the mid-nineteenth century, and which still crosses the stream in the park, was formed by pouring cement into a gutter shaped to look like thick branches of a tree, in which were distributed little pieces of wood to imitate the irregularities of bark. Metal rods were inserted to give strength, and the moulding ensured that the bridge would have the appearance of genuine timber[3].

A number of examples of reinforced concrete rustic-work can still be found around

Concrete simulates the branches of this rustic fence, Buttes Chaumont, Paris

A concrete tree for monkeys to climb, le Jardin des plantes, Paris

The concrete elm at Oakworth had an interior staircase leading to an upper level

the Loire valley, and gate-posts in particular often appear to be made from tree trunks, but upon closer inspection are found to be of concrete.

Traditionally, the botanic gardens of France exist alongside the zoological gardens, where the animal houses are frequently constructed of timber. Sometimes concrete rustic-work with natural or concrete branches is set ornamentally into the rendered brick walls. Dovecots were often built on the roofs of the animal houses, usually in a very decorative manner. The workmen were given some leeway in the designs they used, and at Le Jardin des Plantes, Tours, one innovative decorator inserted several rows of terracotta flowerpots into the walls of the upper storey, creating an unusual and picturesque effect that can still be admired today.

In Le Jardin des Plantes, Paris, there is a splendid example of a tall tree with branches but devoid of foliage, *en beton rustique*; this is used next to a monkey-house for the animals to climb.

It is ironic that the vogue for the rustic picturesque crossed the English Channel from England to France only to return in the form of reinforced concrete (or rather cement, since it contained no gravel). Some features in reinforced concrete still exist in England: at Cliveden, Berkshire (built in 1891 by the 1st Duke of Westminster) and still standing in the corner of the car-park courtyard, a hollow tree of reinforced concrete reaches some twenty feet into the air; it once belched smoke from the boiler of the private gasworks of the estate.

During the late nineteenth century there was a fashion in England for 'natural' landscape in the conservatory, and reinforced concrete was sometimes used to achieve the desired effect. The Parisian designer Aucante devised a scheme at Oakworth House, Keighly, where benches and a summerhouse were constructed of reinforced concrete and, amazingly, in the winter garden a dead and hollow elm, which appeared to have had its branches lopped off, was constructed by the same method. The elm concealed a staircase leading the visitor along a tortuous route to the head of a cascade.[4]

The Victorian industrial age has passed, yet strangely enough we are now incorporating cast-offs of that era in our rustic gardens. Railway sleepers are being ripped up from disused railway tracks and are even available commercially. They are used to make small bridges, steps, or to retain raised beds, and harmonize well with rustic elements in the garden (Plate 30).

7
THE EDWARDIAN RUSTIC GARDEN

Romantic images of glamorous garden-parties, roses and a leisurely rural lifestyle create lingering memories of the Edwardian era. Photographs taken with the new roll film on the new portable camera have since become nostalgic scenes shrouded in a lazy golden haze, created unwittingly by faded sepia tones. Edwardian ladies succumbed to the charm of country gardens and at their country houses and cottages the middle class turned towards 'Arts and Crafts' ideals. The Arts and Crafts Movement held a sentimental concern for a rural way of life, based on a pre-industrial age and the use of hand labour to achieve quality craftsmanship, thus acknowledging the validity of a simple life in countrified surroundings. There was a new trend for topiary, to display the skill of competent craftsmen; ornamental dovecots and sundials were used as sentimental symbols of the country scene; and the 'cosy nook' or 'old-fashioned corner' under a rose-covered rustic arbour was used to provide a sham rural atmosphere in a suburban garden. Even high-street studio photographers felt it necessary to provide fantasy-type scenery for their portraits, and the rustic garden bench, set against a painted sylvan scene, was an almost compulsory studio prop (Plate 31).

There was also a pergola revival at this time, perhaps encouraged by Gertrude Jekyll (1843—1932), who had travelled to Italy where the pergola had been popular since early Roman times. It was taken up as a feature by the Arts and Crafts Movement, who justified its appearance in the English garden because it looked back to the past.

The rustic pergola at Polesden Lacey, Dorking, Surrey, must surely epitomize the beauty of the Edwardian garden in all its lavish splendour. The estate was purchased by Captain, the Honourable Ronald Greville and his wife in 1906, but Captain Greville died two years later and the garden was then cared for by his wife. At her death in 1944 the estate was acquired by the National Trust. A famous hostess, Mrs Ronnie Greville, as she liked to be known, entertained her friends in high Edwardian style and, appropriately, the 900-acre garden provided flowers, fruit, and vegetables for the house, and guests could wander along the walks and enjoy the lavish flowerbeds and borders maintained in the luxurious fashion worthy of an Edwardian garden. They could enjoy the splendid views of the surrounding countryside; take a stroll through the Pinetum; admire the Rock Garden; or even play a game of croquet on one of the spacious lawns.

However, it was the typical English rose garden that delighted guests then, just as it does today. Walking westward from the house, after passing the Ladies' Garden (where Mrs Greville lies buried), one comes upon a pair of wrought-iron gates set into the walls of what, in the nineteenth century, was the old kitchen garden and, venturing within, one suddenly finds oneself overcome by the most bewitching sight:

the rose garden magnificently planted with some 2000 plants in more than 30 varieties of soft, cool colours. The still air is hung with the delicate perfume of roses and lavender, and tempers frayed by the heat of the summer's day are stunned and soothed by the beauty of this overwhelming picture. The garden is divided into quarters by the rustic pergola walks and within each of the four lawns are beds planted with a variety of hybrid roses, both old and new favourites such as yellow-and-pink-tinged 'Peace' (1945), bright-red 'Uncle Walter' (1963) and older 'Mrs John Laing' (1887). An herbaceous border surrounds the whole garden and some perimeter paths are hedged with lavender, making a palette of the softest shades (Plates 32 and 33).

In spite of the hungry chalk soil, Edwardian rambling roses still race over the pergola. Mrs Greville found the soil so poor that in 1938 she had the beds excavated to a depth of 18 inches into the chalk, which was replaced with good-quality loam; unfortunately, there are still some failures and the beds are often replanted.

Previously built in larch, in 1985 the rotting pergola was reconstructed by the Head Gardener, Robert Hall, using treated local pine, which will give an even longer life. However, in spite of the various difficulties encountered over the years, the Rose Garden is never without interest. The rambling roses draping the pergola are in Edwardian shades: soft pink, crimson, yellow, and white rather than the more garish flame and orange hues of some recent varieties. They are all summer flowering except for the pale pink 'New Dawn' (1930), which is a climbing sport from Dr van Fleet, chosen to prolong the display. The ramblers are grown from *Rosa wichuraiana* stock and it is to this they owe the vigorous and supple qualities that make them a good choice for a pergola. They also make a beautiful blanket for an arbour, and can be very useful for covering ugly sheds or outbuildings.

The thatched bridge over the sunken road, at Polesden Lacey, Surrey

Maori Hut at Clandon Park. Overhanging eaves lined with twigs and decorated posts.

'Dorothy Perkins' (1902) and the 'American Pillar' rose (1909) are both summer-flowering ramblers from America which became increasingly popular in Edwardian times. 'American Pillar' has clusters of bright-pink flowers with white centres, and 'Dorothy Perkins' is another pink rose, which has remained extremely popular in spite of being prone to mildew. 'Excelsa' (1909) has light-crimson flowers and, although the shoots are thin, it is extremely vigorous and is also happy growing through trees. 'Sanders White' (1912) is a useful rambler as it will tolerate shade; it has cool pure-white clusters of flowers which are set off to advantage by its bright-green foliage. 'Albertine Barbier' (1950) is creamy white, faintly tinged with yellow, and 'Albertine' (1921) unites the colour scheme with double pink-and-gold flowers.

The surrounding borders have a variety of early-flowering shrubs followed by a galaxy of pretty herbaceous plants. The wisteria covering the water-tower makes a striking feature before the bedding roses come into flower, and when the roses begin to fade and the hedges of lavender 'Hidcote' along the paths are past their best, the late summer clematis begins to bloom.

Mrs Greville chose the garden ornament carefully, and in the centre of the garden, where the pergola walks cross, is a Venetian well-head: a simple marble ornament in a lavish garden. Leaving the garden by a second pair of wrought-iron gates, after passing by the Iris Garden and the Lavender Garden, the next surprise is a thatched bridge. This feature is quite unusual in Britain, but what is more surprising is that it crosses a deep cut concealing an estate road. This scheme was the brain-child in 1861 of Sir Clinton Dawkins, a former owner of Polesden Lacey. There are built-in seats along each side of the bridge, and when sitting there one is almost unware that traffic is passing beneath. This estate road is, in fact, so deep that traffic cannot be seen from the garden at all. The bridge leads to what in Edwardian days was the kitchen garden, but unfortunately barbed wire now blocks the way. However, over the top of the plantation of pine trees beyond, the thatched roof of the Edwardian summerhouse can just be glimpsed. There has been talk of re-opening this part of the garden and it would be a welcome deed, for it was here, when honeymooning in 1923, that the Duke and Duchess of York, later King George VI and Queen Elizabeth, were photographed. So few old rustic buildings now remain it would be a pleasing gesture for it be renovated. King Edward VII, too, stayed at Polesden Lacey, in 1907, and planted a black mulberry tree to mark the occassion.

This garden has seen many changes and today, with the help of mechanical tools, only five staff are necessary, compared with 38 before the First World War, and 14 in 1938. Life for the staff is easier today in more ways than one: at one time there were notices forbidding them to walk upon the lawns; if caught, on the first occasion it cost the culprit a fine of half a crown, with worse to follow, for if disobedient a second time, dismissal was the punishment.[1]

It was in the Edwardian era that the British Empire was consolidated and this was sometimes made evident in the gardens of country houses or suburban villas of those gentlemen who had professional or business interests in faraway places. Earlier it had been fashionable to have a rather bizarre imitation of some primitive foreign hut in the park or garden; and then Swiss Cottages enjoyed a vogue; but by the Edwardian era many people were well travelled, and a genuine interest in other cultures prompted them to bring home an authentic foreign building from some distant land.

One interesting building brought back to England was a Maori Meeting House, or *whare*, from New Zealand, bought by the 4th Earl Onslow on 21 January 1892 for the sum of £25.00. The whare originally came from the foot of the Wairoa Mountains. In 1886 the surrounding countryside was devastated by the eruption of a volcano and earthquake shock waves. Many terrified people took shelter in this single-roomed building, but, almost buried by lava and ashes, it nearly proved to be their tomb. The whare remained partly buried by debris for several years until Lord Onslow, then Governor of New Zealand, had it uncovered and shipped home to the garden of his country house at Clandon Park, Surrey,[2] where it still stands (Plate 34).

It is a very solid building and its single room is protected by a heavy thatch that extends over the front to form a shady porch. The pitch of the thatch is formed by huge beams, some two feet apart, and between these beams, on the underside roof extension, are straight lengths of coppiced poles of about one inch in diameter, laid side by side. The beams of the interior and those of the porch, like the other timbers used in the construction, are highly decorated with primitive paintings of stylized figures in ochre, black, and white matt paint, with details in mother-of-pearl. The front of the building is covered with vertical bamboo canes, and the single room is entered by a sturdy door, painted white. The only light is via a casement window. The floor is covered with raked sand and the walls are lined with rush matting. There is a central vertical timber, a totem pole, carved and painted in the same style as the rest of the building. The carved male figure at the base is a phallic symbol representing fertility, and a lizard slithering down the post from above is also a Maori symbol. The building is set against a background of trees and at the side is a shrubbery, where a pretty acer echoes the colour of this unusual building.

Sir Thomas Lipton, who was 'in tea', had a mansion called 'Ossidge' to the north of London, known for its air of colonialism created by treasures collected by Sir Thomas in South Africa, India, and Ceylon. There was a welcome at the front door from a pair of china negresses, and the billiard room was decorated with lion skins and an elephant's head; there were even porcupine-quill chairs. However, in the garden Edwardian romance lingered: there was trellis work, no doubt rose-covered, and a rustic veranda ran along the entire length of the back of the house; most romantic of all was a summerhouse, built way up in the branches of an old oak tree. Perhaps the idea of constructing a tree-house in his garden in England was conceived in one of the distant lands Sir Thomas had visited, where tree-houses have been part of the landscape for centuries, frequently as a look-out for wild animals. Nevertheless, to take tea served by elegant Singhalese waiters dressed in white, in a tree-house amidst the branches of one of England's most favourite trees, reached by climbing rustic steps winding about its handsome trunk, must indeed have been an elegant occasion. However, it is amusing to see from the photograph that there were two staircases: one obviously the main stairway and the other the back stairs for use by the servants.

However, having come from a poor Irish family, Sir Thomas Lipton was generous to his staff, and in 1884, soon after he had moved into the house, he gave a fantastic garden-party for 500 of his London employees. It was a beano of the best kind: there was festive food and, in the fashion of the day, races were run, but this was a very special occasion and each participant was given a sports card announcing 'The Lipton Cup, to be run for the human race'.[3]

Sir Thomas Lipton's tree-house, Ossidge, Enfield, c.1900

Tree-houses were an essential feature of early Persian gardens and had also been popular in Spain and Italy. In the USA 'Prospect Towers' were built by Andrew Jackson Downing to afford a better view, but in England tree-houses are used mainly as children's play-houses, and it must be said that they seem to have a reputation as places for fun and games. There was a tree-house built in Renaissance Italy that was the cause of a great deal of fun and merriment. This was arranged in a great evergreen oak by the artist Tribolo at the famous garden at Castello. The trunk of the huge tree was thickly entwined with ivy and a wooden staircase, also decorated with ivy, led up into the boughs of the tree to a thickly screened square room surrounded with seats on all sides. So thick was the luxuriant growth that it was almost impossible to see the view, except through apertures formed here and there where branches had been clipped away. In the centre was a little marble table, with a vase of marble in the middle from which a strong jet of water spurted into the air. The copper pipes

Le Bosquet du Restaurant du Vrai Chataignier, Paris where champagne picnics were hoisted on rope pullies by waiters serving the diners in the curtained rendez-vous *high in the tree tops*

that fed this contrivance came up from the foot of the oak, and were carefully concealed by ivy. The water could be turned on or off by means of keys, and the power adjusted. According to fancy, the visitor, taken by surprise, could be dampened, or drenched, and just to add to the fun there were hidden sound effects which produced various sounds and whistlings to astonish the victim yet more. Water jokes of this kind were a feature of Renaissance gardens; visitors could never know quite where or when to expect them and although they were a great source of amusement, a few cross words were exchanged too, no doubt![4]

Centuries later, in 1911, in Paris, tree-houses were used for play of another kind! Romantic Frenchmen delight in telling the story of the tree-houses that formed *Les Bosquets du Restaurant du Vrai Chataignier*, in Robinson Park, Paris. Here, at the turn of the century, lovers spent their Sunday afternoons; they were served by waiters who used pulleys to raise picnic baskets of goodies and champagne for the couples to enjoy in their curtained *rendez-vous* high above.

Restaurants and cafés have always been an important part of the French way of life: a place for social meeting, or just somewhere to pass an idle hour. Perhaps this

Restaurant de l'Ermitage de Villebon, where topiary matched the rustic features

is why the rustic scene was frequently the chosen style of architecture for park restaurants. Topiary is a traditional feature of French gardens, so it is appropriate that at the *Restaurant de l'Ermitage de Villebon*, which is situated in a topiary garden, the rustic features should take on similar shapes to the contorted trees.

In 1797, Grohman, a German, published his design for what he called a *Gesellschafts Linde*, a 'lime tree for a social gathering', or what we might now call a Crow's Nest. A crow's nest is a fairly easy structure to build in the branches of a tree. It comprises a platform enclosed by strongly built railings, and reached by a stair or ladder. A crow's nest is never roofed over as the shade and shelter of the tree's green canopy should be sufficient. Choose the largest of the tree's limbs, or erect strong posts embedded in the ground so that the floor can be laid evenly and firmly. For safety's sake the corner posts and connecting rails must be strong and well secured. If a rustic railing is chosen, lighter decorative pieces must be confined to the spaces between the main rails. Alternatively, the platform can be enclosed with a fence of bark-covered slabs. Winding stairs can be built around the trunk or around the posts, but again, the emphasis must be given to strength. If strong branches are not available, worked wood can soon be disguised by a drapery of vines weaving around the rails. A rustic table and chairs are the only furnishing needed. Now that bird-watching is so popular, a crow's nest could double up as a hide. A series of 'nests', supported by large woodland trees, could be very exciting. The adventurous could climb from one nest to another to encounter a fresh view at every stage.

At the Old Forge, Quality Street, Merstham, Surrey, a ladder reached up to a simple crow's nest resting in a lofty tree, high above the straight hedges and borders, and the raspberry canes that were all typical features of the Edwardian suburban garden. Quality Street was an early eighteenth-century street that was extended at

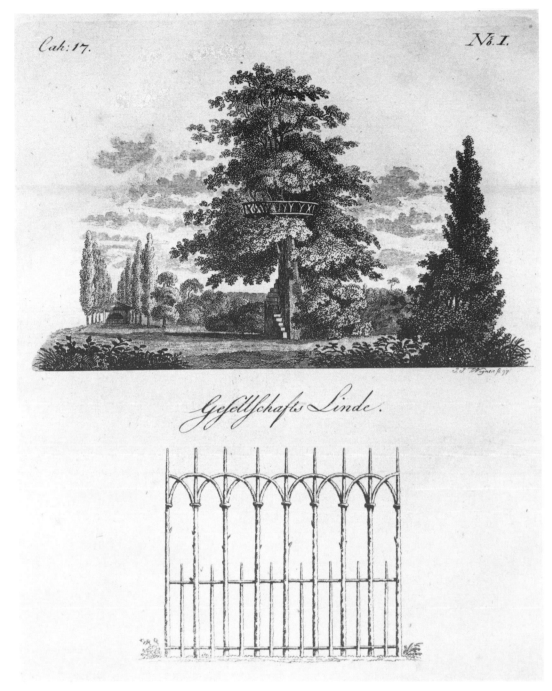

Gesellschafts Linde, Johan Grohmann, 1797

the end of the nineteenth century. Old Forge was the home of Ellaline Terriss and Seymour Hicks whilst they were appearing in Barrie's play *Quality Street*, after which the street was named.

In Edwardian England, there was another kind of rustic garden: the Japanese garden. Visitors to Japan are often bewitched by the tranquility and timelessness of the gardens there. Ancient mossy stones, quiet pools and stepping-stones, tea-houses, and neat fences of bamboo poles carefully knotted together, are all arranged harmoniously with

Japanese tea-house at Heale House gardens, brought back from Japan by the Hon. Louis Greville, 1910

a skill peculiar to the Japanese. In the early twentieth century several gardens were built in the Japanese style by diplomats returning home from Japan. The Japanese garden at Heale House, Wiltshire, fulfilled the dream of the Hon. Louis Greville, great-uncle of the present owner, when he returned from diplomatic service in Tokyo at the turn of the century.

Japanese gardens outside Japan are often found as gardens-within-gardens and this is so with the Japanese water garden at Heale House. It is part of a charming and unpretentious garden which nestles against a curve in the lazy River Avon. A channel of water was diverted to form a water garden and the tea-house, brought back from Japan by Louis Greville, straddles a stream where trout can sometimes be seen jumping in the water passing beneath. It is a charming, but now fragile building, with *shoji* (screens of rice paper) gently diffusing the interior light, and a wooden floor covered with the soft and silky straw matting known as *tatami*. The atmosphere is calm and tranquil; the perfect setting for the Tea Ceremony, an ancient Japanese art form which follows a rigid ritual for making, serving, and drinking tea. In the gentle atmosphere

(Opposite:) The Old Forge, Quality Street, Merstham, home of Ellaline Terris and Seymour Hicks

of the tea-house the participant is able to appreciate a simpler way of life and is brought into closer communication with nature. There are some 100,000 registered teachers of the Tea Ceremony throughout Japan, who train their students in this technique, said to calm the soul, develop aesthetic sensibilities, and so nurture a more refined taste.[6]

Shrubs and trees have been allowed to become larger and fuller than would be permitted in Japan, where gardeners spend endless hours trimming and pruning, but it retains a naturalness which, to Western eyes enhances the scene. Instead of the ponds of an earlier day, streams of water now wind their way around the trees; acers, a liquid amber, and masses of cherry trees, which are a sea of blossom in the spring. Japanese tea gardens do not have many flowers: in the tea-room, within the tea-house, is an alcove, the *tokonoma*, where an arrangement of flowers is displayed in the Japanese style of Ikebana, using very few, or even just one flower. The flowers in the garden are kept to a minimum because they must not compete with the Ikebana.

However, the woodland around the tea-house at Heale is perfect in the spring, when it is lit up by clumps of primulas, scillas, anemones, and bluebells that would seduce even the most faithful Japanese gardener. In 1910, Harold Peto drew up plans for the formal part of the main garden at Heale, and it is possible that he had some involvement with the Japanese garden there. After his visit to Japan in 1889, he introduced Japanese elements into many rock and wild gardens, which were the height of fashion around this time.

Upon his return from Japan, Peto brought the dilapidated Iford Manor in Wiltshire. He had been in partnership with the architect Sir Ernest George, and they were later joined by the young Edwin Lutyens, who was very much influenced by Peto. After travelling abroad Peto became increasingly interested in garden design and accepted many commissions. However, the gardens at Iford Manor, where he lived, are a treasure house of plants and architecture. The architectural fragments which he collected in Italy were arranged at his leisure and displayed in the most appropriate ways. His love of Italy, where he worked on gardens, came to the fore in his own garden, but across an upper terrace and up a stepped pathway is the Japanese garden. It is believed that this garden was started by Peto, but left incomplete at his death in 1933; alternatively, it may just have fallen into a state of disrepair. However, all is not lost, for although many decades have passed (as well as the Second World War, which took its toll on many beautiful gardens) the present owners are courageously putting the Japanese garden back together again. A pagoda there was put in place by Peto, and the bamboos were planted by him, but the present owner is completing the pool and the rest of the garden. The little rustic house is quite different from the tea-house at Heale, and is built with sturdy walls of wide, split timbers standing on a timber plinth. It has a heavy roof of local stone tiles, curving very slightly upward at the eaves. There is a second rustic hut overlooking the kitchen garden, built in a similar style, but larger. It is extremely attractive, built with the same wide split timbers, and a stone-tiled roof flushed with colour by green mosses. The central post is formed by

(Opposite:) Like this Japanese garden at Halton House, Buckinghamshire, Japanese gardens in England were often gardens within gardens

a quaint wooden sculpture of a frowning dwarf-like figure, with thick lips and sad eyes. He is clothed in a smock and clutches a branch while diligently supporting the roof on his capped head, his knees bending under the weight. He surely must have a tale to tell (Plate 35).

Unfortunately, some Japanese gardens were far removed from the real thing, and at Halton House in Buckinghamshire, although described as a Japanese garden, the garden here was little more than a mixture of rustic and gardenesque elements. Nevertheless, it was pretty, and the thatched gazebo is very interesting, as it was marketed by William Cooper Ltd. of south-east London:

> Portable 3-Gabled Thatched-Roof Rustic Summer House, This is one of the most effective designs ever produced for a Summer House. It is a charming adornment to a garden wherever erected. A flight of steps in the centre leads to a balcony platform, which surrounds the house. It is artistically finished both inside and out.
>
> Size 12 ft by 12 ft over all. House, 8 ft by 8 ft, giving 2 ft Balcony all round. Raised 2 ft 6 in off the ground. Price, complete on rail, at our Works, thatched, £42; if boarded roof, £32. This house can be made to any size required. Prices forwarded upon receipt of specification.

Harold Peto may have been involved with the gardens of West Dean, near Chichester, where he and Ernest George were responsible for major alterations to the house between 1891 and 1893. The estate lies at the foot of the Sussex downs, six miles north of Chichester, amidst rolling countryside of woodlands and meadows, and pretty villages of knapped flint and country gardens. It is this pictorial quality that is carried over into the gardens of West Dean. In its Edwardian heyday, West Dean was the home of William James and his vivacious wife Evelyn who, through her wit and charm, became one of the leading hostesses of the 'Marlborough House Set'. In true Edwardian style, West Dean was the venue for many house parties and was another of those houses frequently visited by Edward VII who, as usual, set the pace for modern living by 'motoring down'.

The gardens at West Dean are a contrast of spacious lawns and woodland walks, where the country charm of thatched summerhouses and herbaceous borders sit happily together with the Italianate pergola and formal water garden. There are three different rustic summerhouses. The smallest, recently restored, is simply built and lined with panels of diamond twig-work to the interior. It is covered with a thatched roof and a new floor has been laid made of cut pine logs. It is a very ordinary little hut, but the view from it is delightful: in the foreground is a sunken water garden, which can be enjoyed for its own sake, but, looking out across the water garden, the eye is taken past the house to the rolling downs beyond, where sheep graze and a little white-chalk road is lost in the distance.

Leaving this summerhouse, after wandering under a canopy of very tall and beautiful trees, there is a sweeping lawn across which a huge cedar throws its shadow. On the edge of the lawn is another summerhouse. The rear walls of this summerhouse are built from brick, but the interior is decorated with rustic twig-work, and the floor is a pattern of knapped flints and horses' molars. The front of the summerhouse is formed from attractively shaped branches. The openings on either side of the entrance are trellised to half-way up, leaving an open view across the lawn to the pergola,

Norwegian hut at West Dean.

whose classical stone columns support wooden lintels draped with glorious mauve racemes on the old and gnarled wisteria.

The third and largest summerhouse is reached by a path through a woodland area; it lies tucked back, almost concealed from view by bold shrubs, thick spikes of acanthus, and contrasting red poppies, all jostling with each other for a place in the sunshine. This is a cool shady summerhouse, a perfect place to shelter in the heat of the day, in the quietness of the garden away from the house. It is large enough to take quite a group of people and there are built-in seats all the way round its circular interior. Imagine those light-hearted Edwardians and their *joie de vivre*, laughing and joking, perhaps recalling fun had at a day's racing at nearby Goodwood racecourse.

There is a little stream bubbling and gurgling its way through the woodland of ferns where, in the spring, primroses and daffodils, bluebells and, later, foxgloves grow. It is crossed by several little bridges; some are built in the timber rustic style and others are decorated with tough, but fragile-looking stonework, which is hardly discernible from timber. One bridge has a stone base and a rustic balustrade; another is constructed completely of rough timber and looks as if it could be a recent addition. With the exotic foliage of a palm tree on one bank, and dense evergreens shading the stream on the other, one could be in some distant land. Does this thick cover perhaps echo the days when William James, the owner of West Dean, was famous as a big game-hunter (in one winter alone he killed 35 beasts). There is a collection of lions' heads, some of Willie's trophies, in bamboo and glass cases which still stand in the house, but he gave up hunting when his brother Frank was killed by a wounded elephant in Gabon, in 1890. However, Willie continued to hunt in a smaller way, for the pheasant and partridge shooting at West Dean was considered among the best in the country. He was joined on many occasions by Edward VII, who was a keen shot.

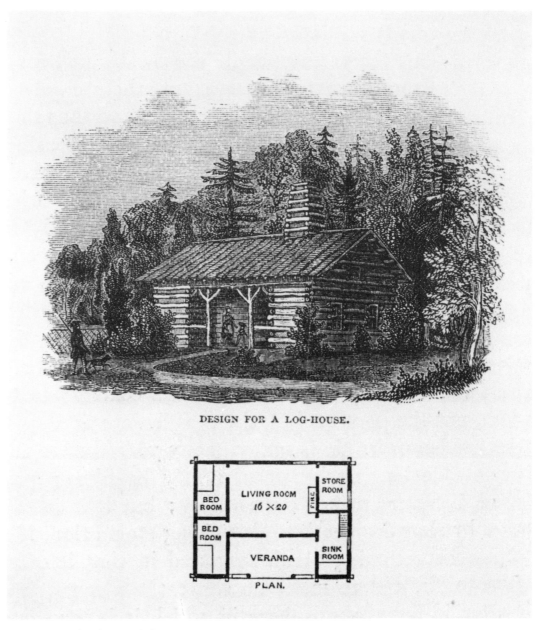

DESIGN FOR A LOG-HOUSE.

Design for a log house, Calvert Vaux, 1874

Edward VII first stayed at West Dean when still the Prince of Wales. It had been his habit to stay at Goodwood House, but when he had a disagreement with the Duke of Richmond, who would not extend his hospitality to two ladies on the Prince's guest list, the Prince declined all future hospitality and chose to stay at West Dean instead. This he continued to do after he came to the throne, and the young Queen Alexandra became a firm friend of the fun-loving Evelyn James.

St Roche's arboretum at West Dean extends over 42 acres. Newly discovered species were added to the existing woodland as they were introduced, and for such poor chalky soil there is a surprisingly large number of lofty conifers, and even flourishing rhododendrons. Tucked away in the arboretum was a shooting lodge — the

'Norwegian Hut'. An enthusiastic sailor, in 1889 William James brought the Norwegian Hut back from Norway on his yacht. In its early days the roof was of turf, but it was later found necessary to replace this.[7] The hut, sadly now demolished, was very skilfully constructed by traditional methods, and so well jointed that it was unnecessary to use any screws or nails.

Log huts are universally found in heavily forested areas, wherever a scarcity of brick or stone prevails, and they are still popular throughout the USA as holiday homes. This tradition started first from necessity and was then continued by those determined to be at one with nature. Wealth and prosperity are often followed by a yearning for a return to nature and the enjoyment of its fruits, and this is precisely what happened in New York State at the turn of the century.

Whilst the rustic tradition flourished in English country gardens, prominent New York citizens, with names like Vanderbilt and Rockefeller, went off to vacation in the Adirondack Mountains (upstate New York) to seek out an outdoor life of hunting and fishing. Although at first they were content to make do with tents and the bark shelters that their industrious guides knocked together for them, they were more accustomed to luxurious living, and it was not long before they were employing their local 'Jack-of-all-trades' guides to erect log cabins. Later, very competent architects were employed to design elaborate rustic lodges which became known as camps. Early buildings were utilitarian, with little or no ornamentation, but gradually, perhaps inspired by trends set by Anthony Jackson Downing, rustic ornament made its mark, and many of the log cabins and camps were decorated inside and out with a variety of rustic embellishments.

A multitude of rustic crafts was used in the construction of these huts, mainly imported from Europe: peeled pole and branch construction, mosaic twig-work, and applied bark as used in Scandinavia and by the North American Indians. Hunting trophies too, were part of the decorative interiors and, as well as fur rugs, stuffed bears, stags, racoons, chipmunks, and squirrels, it was not unusual to find a peeled branch decorated with small stuffed perching birds. A habit which, fortunately, no longer enjoys popularity.

The porch was a feature of most Adirondack camps and, open to the fresh air and sheltered from the weather, it was a useful platform for outdoor living, linking house and garden. A variety of rustic seats and benches, rocking chairs and swings, tables and flower-stands, ensured it was furnished for comfort. All far removed from the primitive life they had at first sought, but still offering a place where one could 'get away from it all'.

8

ROYALTY, WRITERS, AND THE RUSTIC TASTE

Gardens have always been an important aspect of royal life, for it is in their gardens that royalty can escape to a private world away from the ever constant gaze of the public eye. Many members of various royal families around Europe have been captured by the fairyland qualities of rusticity, and chosen to escape to a garden with a rustic theme. Some built pastoral playgrounds where they could lead lives of bucolic fantasy. Royal followers of fashion too, have chosen rustic settings for their private world, and for others, with a more practical outlook, the rustic garden came to play an important part in creating a happy family life.

Writers are another group who have, for various reasons, been captured by the charm of rusticity, and have chosen this as an imaginative escape, where they can write or ponder over poetry or prose. Dr Johnson, William Wordsworth, and Charles Dickens all had rustic summerhouses. Each rustic building was as different as the style of each writer, but it may be that, for each writer, when he retired to his rustic haunt, removed from the real world, the imagination was kindled and words flowed.

The small château and gardens that replaced the village of Trianon, at Versailles, and took the name of that village, were the pride and joy of Louis XIV, but somewhat unusual methods were used to keep the flowerbeds constantly full of colour. The Navy was commanded to keep the garden supplied with plants brought from warmer climates, so that even in the cold winter months of December and January the beds could be crammed full with daffodils and hyacinths. These enormous orders had to be dealt with immediately, and so Le Bouteux, the Head Gardener, kept ready the astronomical number of 1,000,900 flowerpots![1] However, each successive king made his own improvements and, to please Madame de Pompadour, Louis XV built the Petit Trianon. A keen botanist, he extended the gardens, and laid out a potager (kitchen garden) and a botanical garden, where all sorts of vegetables and fruits were grown. Scientific experiments, carried out under the watchful eye of the famous Claude Richard, attracted the attention of botanists from all over Europe. However, upon the death of Louis XV his son made a present of the Petit Trianon to his Queen Consort, Marie Antoinette, marking the beginning of yet another epoch in the garden's history.

The irregular design of the English landscape park was taken up quickly across the Channel, and rustic garden conceits and picturesque cottages, like that of Rousseau at Ermonville, promptly appeared in the *jardins anglais*, as they became known.

In France, the idea of the Swiss Cottage and Russian Lodge was taken a stage further than in England. At Franconville, a complete Swiss Village was built, and at Le Raincy a Russian village. However, it was the *Hameau* at Chantilly, a group of seven thatched houses around a green, built in 1773, that inspired Marie Antoinette to embark on the extravagant scheme for a new garden, and the Hameau at Versailles that was to earn her the name *Madame Deficit*. The superb botanical gardens of Louis XV were swept away and the majority of precious plants transported to Le Jardin des Plantes, Paris. Thus began an expensive project which was to last for more than a decade.

After having plans from various designers, the Queen chose the architect Richard Mique. From 1773 were built a tilting yard, a Chinese pagoda, and artificial rocks with grotto, and alpine walk leading up to the Belvedere. From this elevated position, the Queen was able to admire her new *ferme ornée* where she and her entourage could escape the rigours of court life. It was here that she could lead a life of pastoral fantasy, surrounded by her courtiers who played at being shepherds and shepherdesses.

Concealed in the centre of the wood was the 'Theatre de la Reine', constructed in 1780, where the sovereign produced and performed mini comic operas before her privileged guests; these events came to be associated with various scandals. After the many nocturnal *fêtes*, Marie Antoinette would go to the Temple of Love to rest. The Temple stands on a little island in the midst of lawns that were planted with exotic and rare trees, and the charming setting was completed by a little river that enclosed the island.[2] The Hameau was constructed by Mique around the artificial lake. There was a dairy, and a large barn which served as a ballroom. Some of the farm buildings still remain. The Queen's cottage is two houses connected by a timber gallery, reached by an exterior spiral staircase which wraps itself around a tree to create a rural, though somewhat elegant, rustic style. This was achieved in quite substantial materials, yet decorated to represent an artificial state of dilapidation. The house is the perfect foil for the climbing plants and flowerpots that decorate the gallery. In Marie Antoinette's day the latter were of blue-and-white porcelain bearing the Queen's monogram. This picturesque and rustic charm was only skin deep, for the interior was as sophisticated as any of the rooms of the chateau.

Behind the Queen's house is a little cottage called *le Rechauffoir*, and across the lake the mill completes the stage-set village. The group of 14 cottages, protected by thick tiles or thatch, have pretty rustic porches of what appears to be worm-eaten timber which cast interesting shadows on the old brick and plasterwork walls. Each cottage has its own garden enclosed by quaint rustic fences. In summertime one is a colourful mass of golden dahlias; most endearing is a picturesque *potager*, planted with rows and rows of ornamental coloured cabbages, tucked in behind a low box hedge. Cabbages are a large family and the ornamental variety has a central ball with leaves that break into a crinkly froth of white or pink. The ball of tightly growing leaves is said to symbolize happiness and prosperity. However, alchemists believed that sulphur in a body was what the sun is to the universe, and the high sulphur content of cabbage was therefore associated with self-centred egotism in those who ate them. Is the choice of cabbages for these gardens perhaps something to do with the history of the place?

The Hameau at Versaille was admired by Queen Charlotte, wife of George III of England. When an Act of Parliament granted Her Majesty the Frogmore estate she set out to captivate the charm of the Picturesque by creating a rural playground, not unlike that at Versailles. There was a thatched barn where dances were held, a thatched hermitage designed by her daughter Princess Elizabeth, and a cornmill, in accord with a concern for self-sufficiency, as well as temples and Gothic ruins. There were *fêtes-champetres* held to honour royal occasions, but Queen Charlotte spent more and more

Le Hameau de la Reine, Versailles. The rural retreat of the Queen Consort, Marie Antoinette

of her time at Frogmore enjoying a simple and peaceful life. She found many of her pleasures in the gardens: botany was a favourite pastime and she was an ardent collector of plants. Some came from Kew and many came from other sources around the world. In the hermitage she would spend time drawing and drying plants, and would wander through the grounds, either on foot or riding her donkey, admiring and watching the development of her plants (Plate 39). The landscape has changed little over the centuries, although other follies and garden buildings have been added. By the lake is a typical Victorian rustic summerhouse, known as the Canadian Hut. This, sheltered by a yew hedge, is constructed in brick with a slate roof, but embellished inside and out in the rustic style. The exterior walls are decorated with a criss-cross design of split pine. The front façade has a pediment of pine logs supported by rustic tree-trunk piers. The interior has been decorated with a mosaic of branches arranged to form a series of arched gothic panels picked out in silver birch, and the ceiling of bark slabs has a central rose of fir-cones and birch encircling a grotesque tree butt.

Osborne was the perfect home for Queen Victoria and her family. Here, they could enjoy privacy, and walk anywhere without being followed and peered at. Prince Albert, a countryman at heart, could escape Court society and the bustle of the city, and the landscaping of the estate offered a challenge which he readily took up.

The house stands in undulating landscape on the north-eastern shore of the Isle of Wight. There are still spacious lawns leading down to the sea, and the views from the house are enlivened by the white sailing boats that glide across the blue waters of the Solent. Queen Victoria loved the sea and was pleased by the small private beach that could be reached by a path through the woods to where the trees grew right down to the water's edge.

Summerhouse at Frogmore Gardens, Windsor

The landscaping, carried out largely under Prince Albert's supervision, paid particular attention to the needs of the children, and is a reflection of the happy family life that they must have enjoyed at Osborne. At first, the grounds were in a rough state, but were soon sown with grass to become a playground for the royal children. The Prince Consort enthusiastically planted a variety of trees, including evergreen oaks, Scotch firs, cork oaks, and stone pine. Specimen trees were planted to mark the visit of any important persons, birthdays, and other special occasions. A profusion of climbing plants were chosen to grow against the kitchen wall. Heather decorated the terraces and a belt of evergreen shrubs was planted. At some distance from the house the children were given their own little garden, and these were planted, and, to a large extent, cultivated by them, with their own little tools. Each had a miniature spade, hoe, and wheelbarrow, marked with the initials of the royal owner. These tools are still neatly stored in their original thatched shed along with the dogcart in which the youngest children would sometimes ride. If any of the children cultivated a good vegetable plot, he or she would be rewarded with a certificate from the under-gardener. This was given to Prince Albert, who would then buy the produce from the child at the current market price.

Detail of the summerhouse at Frogmore Gardens. The building is built of brick with an embellishment of logwork both inside and out

With the children in mind, another building appeared in this part of the garden: Queen Victoria was concerned that the children should have more privacy, and in 1854 a Swiss chalet was erected about three-quarters of a mile away from the house. This feature was prefabricated in Switzerland and came complete with an external gallery and staircase, on which are carved proverbs. These are in German, but the translation is as follows:

south side: Keep the head cool, the feet warm,
that makes the best doctor poor.

If your work does not succeed you must compel it by perseverence.

Quickly attempted is half won.

west side: On God's blessing all is dependent,
who trusts God has built well.

north side: Much more easily will you carry what you carry,
if you put patience to the burden

Our outgoings may God bless, our coming in equally guide.

east side: Early to bed, early to rise,
makes a man healthy, wealthy and wise.

The Swiss chalet was rather like a schoolhouse and fitted up with every convenience for the children's practical training in domestic management. On the ground floor the girls had cookery lessons: simple dishes were prepared using the bright copper utensils, and served on charming Wedgwood china. The upper floor was simply furnished with furniture of light wood, including a cradle for the youngest child. Prince Albert was fond of carpentry and a workshop was installed for the boys where he was able to pass on his practical skills.

Close by the Swiss chalet a natural history museum was built, in a similar style, to house the many curiosities, botanical and geological specimens, collected and arranged mainly by the children themselves, and supplemented by gifts from home and abroad. The collection is still there to be admired and confirm the happy times that the royal children must have had in their own part of the estate.

Sandringham has long been a favourite country home of the Royal Family, and it was here that a dairy was built, modelled on Queen Victoria's Swiss Cottage at Osborne. This dairy was to become a favourite place of Queen Alexandra, where members of the Royal Family and their friends would be entertained for tea as they looked out over the sunken garden, which contained a number of yews and box trees cut to resemble armchairs, boats, birds and snakes curling up sticks! There were two sundials in the gardens, one made from part of the old Kew Bridge. Edward, Prince of Wales installed 'Sandringham Time', whereby all clocks were kept half an hour fast to extend the daylight hours of shooting days. This practice continued until his death and many years later, in 1950, Quen Mary erected a statue of Father Time, that stands in the garden gazing towards the house.

Horse-racing has often been described as the 'sport of kings' and the Prince of Wales was no exception in his enjoyment of this sport. His horse Persimmon won the

The royal children's tool shed, Osborne

The Swiss Cottage, Osborne where the royal children took lessons

Derby, the Jockey Club Stakes and the St Leger in 1896, and the Eclipse Stakes and the Gold Cup in 1897; the Prince joked that the horse was paying for work in the Sandringham gardens. An extensive sweep of teak greenhouses were built (perhaps out of race winnings) and dedicated to the horse: they were called 'the Persimmon range'.[3]

The Sandringham gardens soon became very Edwardian. The rosary of arched bowers around a central fountain were planted with all the Edwardian favourites, a thatched summerhouse replaced the pavilion, and rustic seats were placed here and there.

The Prince of Wales was very fond of the gardens and after he became King Edward VII he is said to have remarked to Admiral 'Jacky' Fisher that if he could have chosen his own career he would have been a landscape gardener.

Queen Alexandra too was very fond of the gardens, and after the King's death she spent a great deal of her time at Sandringham, attended by her lady-in-waiting Charlotte Knollys. The Comptroller-General, Sir Dighton Probyn, was never far away and, devoted to Queen Alexandra, he referred to her as 'The Blessed Lady'. By the lake was a grotto, or boathouse, formed with large boulders of local stone, and on the rockery above Probyn had a little summerhouse built for the Queen as a token of his affection, with an inscription reading:

Albert Edward, Prince of Wales, and Alexandra, Princess of Wales, Sandringham, April, 1863

'The Queen's Nest' — A small offering to The Blessed Lady from Her Beloved Majesty's very devoted old servant General Probyn, 1913 — To-day, to-morrow and everyday God bless and guard her I fervently pray.

Dr Samuel Johnson (1709–1784) enjoyed a close friendship with the famous Thrale family, and when he suffered a severe nervous breakdown the Thrales visited him at his home in Johnson Court and then took him back to their home in Streatham to nurse him back to health. During their many years of friendship Dr Johnson spent much of his time staying with them, becoming virtually a member of the family. The vogue for the picturesque was in full swing in Dr Johnson's lifetime and he joined the Thrales in a visit to Wales going on to enjoy a visit to Hawkstone. He was critical, however, when an avenue of oaks was cut down to comply with the mode of the picturesque, and summed up his opinion of hermits in the following verse:

The bench of mosaic twig-work runs along the eight sides of Dr Johnson's Summerhouse at Kenwood (destroyed by fire, May 1991)

Hermit hoar, in solemn cell,
Wearing out life's evening gray;
Smite thy bosom, sage, and tell,
What is bliss, and which the way?
Thus I spoke; and speaking sigh'd;
— Scarce repressed the starting tear; —
When the smiling sage reply'd —
Come, my lad, and drink some beer.[4]

There were grounds of some hundred acres around the Thrale home at Streatham Park, and one of Johnson's favourite retreats was the little thatched summerhouse, where he may well have spent time writing, and enjoying nature.

By 1826, long after Johnson's death, the family interest in the house ceased; the summerhouse was purchased by Susannah Arabella Thrale and moved to the garden of her home near Knockholt, Kent, where it remained until 1962. By this time it was in a derelict condition, but it was saved from destruction when it was purchased by William Henry Wells of Beckingham, who presented it to the London County Council. The little summerhouse was restored, and after some discussion as to whether it should stand in the churchyard of St Paul's Cathedral, where Johnson worshipped, it was eventually erected in the grounds of Kenwood House, Highgate (Plate 40)[5].

It is a pretty, octagonal, thatched summerhouse, with deep overhanging eaves lined with short lengths of twigs. It may once have had windows, but now the whole of the interior, including the ceiling, is decorated with mosaic twig-work arranged in patterns of diamond and fan shapes. There is a bench fitted round the interior, and this too, is decorated with mosaic twig-work.

William Wordsworth (1770–1850) and his family went to live at Rydal Mount, near Ambleside in the Lake District, on May Day 1813, and remained there until his death in 1850. As well as a poet, Wordsworth also considered himself gifted as a landscape gardener. Indeed he was, for as well as Rydal Mount and Dove Cottage, a previous home, he landscaped Coleorton Hall for his patron, Sir George Beaumont. It is said locally that he landscaped several more gardens for friends and neighbours and all have been admired.

Mount Rydal, originally a yeoman-style cottage, was mentioned in the parish registers of 1574 and the gardens spread for four-and-a-half acres across the lower slopes of Nab Fell. It was here, with the help of his sister Dorothy, that Wordsworth was to create the garden which still remains much as it was in the poet's day, and has been constantly visited and enjoyed by generations of visitors. Dorothy Wordsworth said, 'Rydal Mount is the nicest place in the world for children'[6], and for Wordsworth's seventy-fourth birthday there was a party for 300 guests, many of them children, who had tea in the garden. A visit was also made by Queen Adelaide, widow of William IV, and it was Wordsworth who showed her to the principal points of view. Wordsworth and his sister held a great reverence for nature. Day or night, they loved to roam the countryside around their Cumbrian home, revelling in the majesty of the fells, admiring the tiniest of flowers and creatures, and listening to the pervading sound of the becks and falls: 'the hills, the stars and the white waters with their ever varying yet ceaseless sound'.[7]

Wordsworth despised flamboyant planting, and preferred that his gardens lie

Ceiling rose of Dr Johnson's summerhouse, completely lined with mosaic twig-work (destroyed by fire, May 1991)

within the natural order of things, in harmony with the surrounding countryside. Not for him the bold colours of carpet bedding; his favourites were simple Chaucerian flowers, and the stray yellow poppies or pale primroses that appeared uninvited were welcome visitors. Exotic plants were few and planted, as Wordsworth thought appropriate, near the house.

Rough stone-walled terraces built from local stone and clothed with moss and lichen appear to have grown naturally, as part of the landscape. The first terrace that Wordsworth worked upon was the Sloping Terrace, which is some 250 feet long. Slate steps lead from the house to the walk, which gently rises to a summerhouse built by Wordsworth himself from local materials. The walls are of roughly hewn stone, the floor of cobbles, and the interior is lined with a mosaic of rough pine branches. It is said that the poet would pace up and down the terrace at night composing his verses, and inside the hut he may have found solace. A door on the far side of the summerhouse led to the Far Terrace, and from the path Wordsworth could gaze upon Rydal Water below, shining like silver in the moonlight, and framed by trees carefully planted so as not to obscure the view. When the Queen Dowager visited Rydal Mount she too followed the path through the summerhouse and enjoyed the surprise vista that suddenly unfolds before the visitor. This was one of Wordsworth's favourite walks, and of the terrace he wrote:

> A poet's hand first shaped it; and the steps
> Of that same Bard — repeated to and fro
> At morn, at noon, and under moonlight skies
> Through the vicissitudes of many a year —
> Forbade the weeds to creep o'er its grey line.

Close by the house, Wordsworth bought a field that could be entered through the local churchyard. He was to have had a house built there, but when Dora, his favourite daughter, died in 1847, Wordsworth (then aged 77) and his wife Mary planted the field with daffodils as a living memory of the girl. The bulbs have multiplied and in spring it is a yellow carpet, the 'host of golden daffodils' of the poet's famous poem. Below the Sloping Terrace spreads the woodland, where narrow pathways turn, little streams topple over the natural rockery, and ferns and ivies grow in the dappled shade.

Leaving the woodland, a gravel path passes the sloping lawn surrounded with copper beech, gnarled magnolias, and azaleas and rhododendrons. On one side of the lawn a border of the traditional plants loved by Wordsworth are arranged with painterly skill: daffodils, primroses, polyanthus, and hellebores bloom in the spring; and in summer Sweet Williams, hostas, peonies, and Solomon's Seal spill on to the path. However, it would be unfair to give William Wordsworth all the credit for the planting scheme, for Dorothy's diaries show that she was no less involved in selecting and planting the plants — at times, even by moonlight (Plate 41).

In front of the house are steps leading to 'The Mound', believed to have been a Norse look-out post dating from the ninth century; this was raised still higher by Wordsworth. Banked by rhododendrons and heather, and encircled by a low hedge of oak and beech, this was a favourite spot. It was here that Wordsworth wrote 'Evening Ode' in 1818, and where the family would take tea with their visitors, enjoying the splendid views of Rydal Water to one side, and Windermere on the other, both receding into the distant haze.

Charles Dickens' Swiss Chalet now stands in the garden of Eastgate House, Rochester, (the Nun's House of Edwin Drood). The lion in the centre of the veranda is the lion of Dickens' bookplate

Charles Dickens (1812–1870) lived in several different houses during his lifetime, but his favourite home was Gad's Hill, near Higham, between Rochester and Gravesend. He had admired this house since he was a child and finally bought it in 1855.

It was a large house and had a large garden, with an orchard, and spacious lawns. Evergreen laurels grew against the house walls, and the garden was bright with chrysanthemums, azaleas, primulas, and burning bush and, of course, the Victorian favourite, geraniums, regimented into tidy beds cut into the lawn. Dickens was fond of the garden and if he was away from home he would send instructions to the gardener, Mr Brunt. Dickens referred to one part of the 26 acres as 'The Wilderness'. This was once the term applied to an enclosed wild or woodland garden, but as time went on, in order to create an atmosphere of mystery and bewilderment, grottoes, ruins, waterways, and underground passages became part of the scene. By Victorian times the wilderness was often little more than a shrubbery, but, appropriately, Dickens' brother Alfred built a tunnel, entered by steps from the front lawn, that went under the road to this part of the garden.

It was in the wilderness that in 1865, Dickens chose to erect the Swiss Chalet, a gift from his friend Charles Fetcher, the actor. The chalet was built from 94 separate pieces, which arrived at Higham Station in over 50 packing cases. Before work could begin, space had to be cleared in the wilderness and a foundation laid, but finally the packing cases were transported to the site. These improvements were a costly business, for in having the tunnel built and the chalet erected, Dickens employed 27 men.[8]

However, both time and money were well spent, for Dickens furnished the upper room of the chalet as a study. He wrote four of his most important novels at Gad's Hill, and it was here that, after writing the final pages of *The Mystery of Edwin Drood*, he laid down his pen for the last time.

9

MODERN TRENDS

The prevalence of rustic features at the flower festivals and floralies that have become part of modern leisure is evidence of how popular the rustic style still is. Due to the ravages of time many old rustic features have been lost or destroyed, but some have been restored, and new rustic features, in both contemporary design and reproduction of older styles, continue to appear in our parks and gardens. Rustic bridges can still be found in country gardens; patterns for Swiss cottages are now available off the peg; and rustic summerhouses, like the honey-house in a garden on the edge of the New Forest, continue to be built for a dual purpose (Plate 43).

Some garden owners still look to the past for rustic designs, and may even go so far as to seek out genuine reproductions of antique rustic features. In the garden at Scotlands Farm, Wargrave, Berkshire, a rustic pavilion from an old design has found the perfect site. In 1825, John Adey Repton (1775–1860), son of Humphry Repton, drew a design for a rustic pavilion, and more than 150 years later it was constructed for 'The Garden' exhibition held at the Victoria and Albert Museum, London. Since then the pavilion built from this design has stood at the head of the large pond at Scotlands Farm, in the garden of Mr Michael and The Hon. Mrs Michael Payne (Plate 44).

A series of transformations have taken place at Scotlands since 1976, and the one that first strikes the visitor is the large pond, which was excavated partly as a way to cut down on mowing. Cut down on mowing it did, but the pond created many other tasks to take its place. However, all the hard work was worthwhile; the planting is now mature, and the pond looks as though it has been there forever.

The planting at Scotlands is luxuriant, but one side of the pond has been left as a grassy bank and the water surface remains clear, and can mirror the graceful reflections of the trees and clouds as they silently drift across the sky. Golden orfe glide just beneath the surface of the water, and the tranquility is disturbed only by the moorhens as they scoot hither and thither over the surface. The pavilion takes pride of place at the head of the pond; built of pine logs and decorated with fir-cones, it provides an enchanting spot to sit and enjoy the view, and makes an enchanting focal point. Nearby, the magnificent architectural leaves of gunnera unfurl day by day, until they finally become so gigantic that they dominate the water's edge, providing a foil for the feathery plumes of pink and white astilbes.

Encouraged by the success of this pond, Mrs Payne had two smaller ponds excavated beneath the tall Scots pines in the woodland garden beyond the pavilion. Water tumbles over the rocks on one side of the larger pond, and bluebells and primroses have appeared where brambles were pulled out. There is a profusion of woodland plants, and the pretty scene can be admired from an old rustic bench.

Trees are beautiful, dead or alive: a tree struck by lightening or even Dutch elm disease can make a dramatic silhouette upon a landscape. It was perhaps this sort of scene that centuries ago inspired William Kent, the landscape designer well known for the theatrical effects he created in gardens. It was said by Robert Walpole that Kent was laughed out of his idea of planting dead trees in the garden at Kensington, but perhaps his idea was not as ludicrous as it at first sounds; who knows how the final effect of his dramatic landscape may have looked? After all, the Victorian stumpery used dead roots, tree butts, and pieces of tree trunk, and current trends encourage the use of fallen trees. Woodlands can be severely damaged in great storms, and many gardeners are anxious to have the huge trunks cleared as soon as possible. However, with our growing concern for the environment, some people like to leave a fallen tree or two *in situ*, so that insects are not robbed of their natural habitat. It may not be practical to leave a huge trunk where it fell, but an old tree trunk, carefully placed, or perhaps a butt in a small garden, could become a modern equivalent of the Victorian stumpery, if the surrounding area is treated as a wild garden. A home for wild flowers, collecting moss and fungi, it could create an unusual feature. Alternatively, if you are left with a tidy tree stump in your garden, it can make an attractive seat and, with the addition of a roof, a pretty shelter (Plate 45).

Bridge over a burn in a pretty garden at Lauder in the Border Country

'Alpine', a modern gardenhouse for storage and play

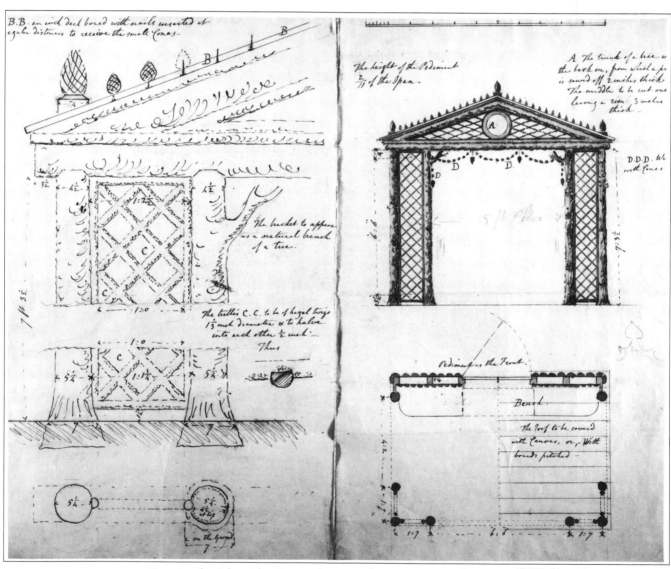

Drawing by John Adey Repton for a pavilion, 1825, recently constructed and standing in the garden of Scotlands, Wargrave. (See also front cover and Plate 44)

Rustic tree shelter, Fanhams Hall, Ware, Hertfordshire

'Alligator crawling from a lake', Parnham

Through the ages sculpture has been especially designed for gardens and gardens have been especially designed for sculpture, but today we are no longer restricted to stone urns and lead statuary. Modern artists and craftsmen work in a variety of mediums, particularly timber: a reflection of the modern attitude that the environment, and all it contains, is considered but a temporary resource.

The work of Madeline Goold must be among the most innovative of any garden sculpture to be found today, and it is totally at home in the rustic garden. Madeline uses no tools and starts each piece of work with a single willow wand and gradually builds up the form to whatever size is appropriate to her subject and the site where it will stand. Her patterns are the drawings she makes in parks, railway stations, markets, and other busy places. The drawings are quick, often just a mass of nervous lines, and the supple willow enables her to make a three-dimensional equivalent.

As they stand in the garden Madeline's sculptures become inhabited by both insects and plants: wrens nested in one figure's head! The figures respond to the seasons, with dried leaves clinging to them in autumn and snow shrouding them in winter. Willow has a life, an ageing and a decline; watched over the years, as they stand in a garden, the figures too appear to have a life, and death, of their own (Plate 46).

Many landscape parks still remain in Great Britain, and several have undergone careful restoration; others have become golf courses, theme parks, or country clubs,

(Opposite:) David Kemp's 'Ancient Forester' at Grizedale Forest, Cumbria, was also exhibited at the Glasgow Garden Festival

but sadly, many have been allowed to deteriorate, or have been destroyed by new roads, property development, or even vandalism. However, time brings change, new ventures evolve, and in the 1990s there is much interest in rustic sculpture, and in the construction of new rustic buildings. Now that land is held at such a premium, gardens are getting smaller and smaller, but, nevertheless, there are alternative open spaces. 'Grizedale Forest Sculpture Project', Cumbria, can be looked upon as the modern equivalent of the landscape park, there for everyone to enjoy. The Sculpture Project is unique; it was established in 1977 to provide a working environment for sculptors, who are given artists' residences under a scheme operated by permission of the Forestry Commission. Working within a working production forest, the sculptor can work in natural surroundings and use natural materials.

Successive sculptors have built up an exciting collection of work; they show a refreshing diversity of approach, reflected in the subject matter and in the use of materials mainly culled from the forest. The sculptures are located at intervals around the nine-and-a-half mile Silurian Way. Visitors are invited to follow the marked trail, to share the experience of the sculptors and to quietly contemplate the sculpture.

The subject matter is varied, ranging from the practical to the fantastic; one could say that they evoke similar emotional responses as the two kinds of beauty described by Edmund Burke in 1757: the smooth, delicate, and harmoniously 'Beautiful' versus the violent, gloomy, and savage 'Sublime'.

At one end of the main car-park at Grizedale (there are several along the trail, which are very useful for disabled visitors) looms the gigantic 'Ancient Forester' made at Grizedale by David Kemp in 1988, and exhibited at the Glasgow Garden Festival. Leaning on his huge axe, this Green Man looks ready to attack anyone who is careless enough to drop litter, light fires, or misuse the forest in any way. A frantic 'Wild Boar', one of a drift of ten made from twigs, mud, and roots, bristles as he roots and scratches in a clearing, recalling images of the wild boar that roamed the medieval forests. A 'Viking Burial Boat' fashioned from wood, stone, earth, and turf, solemnly rests, half-sunken in a hill, within the sound of the running water of a beck tumbling just below. The awesome, architectural 'Seven Spires' reaching upwards to pierce the canopy of the forest, were created in 1984 by Andy Goldsworthy. Slithering and twisting over rocks and through the trees into a clearing is Andy Goldsworthy's huge serpent-like 'Sidewinder', which is 60 yards long. Jim Partridge, a practical man, has carried out functional schemes for a walkway beside a stream, and a bridge, which as well as being useful have a certain beauty of form. The bridge, which spans a small stream, gives wheelchair access to another path. This bridge has low walls moulded from piles of oak logs which were cut from the durable heartwood of trees felled and left for several years until the bark and sapwood had rotted off. It is a beautiful piece of architecture, and a bridge that any great landowner would have been proud to have in his landscape park (Plate 47).

'Private Meeting' (1981) is a group of three standing figures, carved in oak by Robert Koenig, whose theme is Ancestral Man, forest dweller when the forest itself was a source of food gathering, tool and weapon making and shelter. The sculptor

(Opposite:) 'Private Meeting', carved in oak by Robert Koenig

The Whitehorse Woodcraft Shop, Brokerswood, Wiltshire, sells DIY packs of rustic furniture

believes that a group of three helps to create a more complete environment than a single figure.

Grizedale Forest is a constantly changing scene, new works are often added and others are occasionally removed for repair; it is always full of interest, and the 50 or so sculptures offer a rewarding experience to those seeking to enjoy the landscape from a fresh point of view.

At Woodland Park, a working woodland at Brokerswood, in Wiltshire, not only is there a nature trail, but also the White Horse Woodcraft Shop, which specializes in the construction of garden furniture and features and will also supply DIY packages. At this workshop, with its clownish rustic frontage, rustic features for the nearby woodland are built. There are rustic tables and seats in the picnic areas by the lake where the ducks beg an obligatory snack, and in play areas, one may see both children and peacocks using the swings. The old term 'Swing Gardens' belies the coldness of iron swings and roundabouts, and the lawns that children were forbidden to play upon, but cold, hard iron is now being replaced by timber constructions which are warm and comfortable; able to offer adventure to the boisterous ten-year-old, as well as the youngest and most timid of children.

Adventure playgrounds of crude yet well-designed log structures have been built

This slide is part of the 'Menagerie of Animal Magic' designed by Andy Frost in the children's play park at Grizedale

Spider's web with spider watching trespassers, Grizedale

since the 1960s, in local city parks and, in Great Britain, as tourist attractions on aristocratic estates. At Grizedale children have not been neglected and here is one of the most attractive play areas to be found in England. Andy Frost has designed and built a menagerie of animal magic. The slide is down the back of a huge bird, there is a tree house on stilts, and a hedgehog with prickles of logs. The climbing frame is a spider's web slung between two 'fir trees' and a huge spider lurks on the grass watching the trespassers. When it is time to eat, a picnic can be enjoyed while sitting on a toadstool at a toadstool table, while giant ladybirds climb on the neat branches that decorate the wall behind.

More traditionally, in the corner of a green field at Old Warden, Northamptonshire is a swing garden totally in keeping with the picturesque village, with swings, slide, and Wendy house all made of straight pine logs. These are designs that can easily be copied for the garden at home.

Furzey Gardens, Minstead, in the New Forest, is a rustic garden with something for everyone. The eight acres of gardens lie behind a thatched forest cottage believed to have been built in 1560. Carefully restored, the cottage is now open to the public. The garden is on a south-facing hillside, with views over the New Forest to the Isle of Wight. It was designed by Hew Dalrymple, and laid out in 1922 on what was once rough gorse-covered grazing land; subsequently the forest clay was supplemented by cartloads of soil brought in by horse.

Lawns sweep down from the cottage to the informal beds where masses of plants, both great and small, of both vivid and gentle hues, merge together in kaleidoscopic array. Grass paths meander through massed mounds of mature azaleas, and the many rare rhododendrons are a joy in spring, together with the drifts of daffodils, leucojums, erythroniums, fritallarias and camassias. Weed-killers and pesticides are forbidden, so wild flowers are abundant. Wild strawberries grow as ground cover, bluebells surround an old timber seat, and spikes of self-seeding foxgloves brighten dark corners. Dozens of purple orchids litter the woodland glades in spring, so mowing is carried out with care. There is a wide range of heathers, and heather has been used to thatch a round, rustic shelter in the garden. Beneath the thatch, the shelter, partly built with woven-willow panels, is divided into four, to provide separate gossip corners (Plate 48). The favourite view is over the lake; a flowering water garden. Flowering and foliage plants thrive both on the banks and in the water, where golden orfe, golden rudd and mirror carp swim beneath the surface, and a few roach keep the bottom clean. There is a collection of European birch trees growing by the lake, and at the other end of the gardens a *Betula papyrifera*, a native of North America, reaches a height of over 61 feet, and is recorded by the Royal Horticultural Society as being one of the tallest in the country. This species is sometimes known as the 'canoe' birch because it was long ago used by North American Indians for their canoes; or alternatively 'paper' birch, because its bark can be peeled off in large sheets. It is these sheets that are so useful for the bark veneer of rustic-work. Other specimen trees from around the world benefit from the sheltered position of the garden and, along with the winter-flowering shrubs, give interest throughout the year.

One comes upon other rustic features unexpectedly around the garden; two of the prettiest are a round open arbour draped with wisteria and honeysuckle, and a pergola of rough-hewn branches clothed with climbers, containing small alcoves where rustic benches stand. In a distant corner of the garden is a treat for the children: beneath a clump of lofty pines is a little village of miniature, rustic-log cabins and one little hut has a crow's nest above the roof. There is a little of the child in every adult and perhaps it is in such rustic houses that childhood dreams can be realized by adults.

To be the owner of a tree-house must be the ultimate dream of every child who builds his own private den where he can escape from the 'grown-ups'; several grown-ups have built themselves tree-houses where they can escape not only the children, but the rest of the world. The dream of building a tree-house is not often realized but, nurtured on tales of Winnie the Pooh and the palm-fringed tree-house of the Swiss Family Robinson, it is not surprising that several enthusiastic modern spirits have fulfilled their childhood dream and built themselves a tree-top hide-away.

To reach his castle in the air, perched high in the boughs of a 140-year-old ash tree and to enjoy the magnificent views across the Wiltshire countryside, Mark Wilkinson has to climb a 30-foot ladder. Constructed from the trunk of a willow tree

felled by the Electricity Board when laying a new cable, and rescued by Mark, the tree was stripped of its ivy robe and split down the middle to give two matching sides for the ladder. His 16-feet high tree-house is built from a combination of larch, a low quality fencing material, and offcuts from his furniture factory. Great pains were taken to ensure that no damage was done to the tree itself: the house has been built to accommodate the shape of the branches, and spaces left to allow the tree to grow.

At the end of a month of hard work Mark had completed his 'conservationist's folly' and now, in addition to escaping the endless demands of his nearby furniture business, he can often be seen taking drinks on the verandah, having candle-lit dinners with friends, or giving afternoon tea to a stream of fascinated visitors, in elegant style made possible by 'all mod cons'. There is mains running water, electricity for light and heat, a fridge and, the ultimate comfort, a bed that can be made warm by sheets and blankets stored in a heated box (Plate 49).

In spite of these luxuries, the interior of this penthouse has something of the charm of the ornamental hermit's cell. The built-in kitchen has a sink formed from artificial stone, and the fridge has panels of cleft hazel twigs. The gate-leg table is of oak, limed to give it a frosty finish, and a rush-seated chair is made with old barrel staves. There are rope-hung shelves for collected treasures, and a long row of books and bottles, for grey days, line the windowsill.

Considerable thought has been given to the windows which might be described as both 'ancient and modern'. One is of plastic, shaped to fit into the triangular space between the tree's branches, and sealed with rubber adhesive that stops it breaking when the tree moves; another is a small salvaged lattice window, bearing a coat of arms in coloured glass; and a third is Victorian Gothic. However, a surprise comes after dark, when a glass chandelier, made from the necks of 150 wine bottles, secured with chicken wire to a flower-basket frame, filters green and brown light from a halogen lamp.

This tree-house is a splendid achievement that has given a lot of fun to the builder and visitor alike, and perhaps we can look forward to the achievement of Mark's next ambition, which is to build a tree-top restaurant in the grounds of a stately home.

Rusticity never fails to take man into a world of the imagination and the rustic garden is as popular as ever. Old ideas are revived, new ideas evolve, but thatch is something that has become associated with the rustic garden, and wins the heart of everyone who has a yearning to create a rustic scene. Patterns tend to vary from region to region, as they are often passed from father to son, or from one local man to another. Some features seem destined to serve particular countries. The lich-gate, even with a thatched roof, is not popular in England as it is associated with the gateway to the churchyard, where coffin awaits clergyman's arrival. And woe betide anyone who has a single entrance, erects a roofed gate, and then decides to move house (will the furniture have to be left behind?)! However, this is a traditional feature in northern France and occasionally built in the USA.

It is surprising that the 'floral' roofs of Japan and France have not been more

(Opposite:) Pale wisteria and deep-mauve iris complement each other at Furzey Garden, Minstead

widely copied. To see blue and white iris in France, or red lilies in Japan, blooming along the ridges of the sombre-coloured thatch is a delightful spectacle. It is easily achieved by forming soil pockets in the thick straw of the ridge to support the blooming plants, and even if most of us are too conservative to try this on the roofs of our houses, to imitate this idea on our garden buildings would be a great novelty.

Fencing around or within a garden is seldom given much thought, and any concern is usually for its practical attributes rather than how pretty it will be. As a result, fencing is often a very boring selection of mass-produced fencing panels supported by concrete posts. John 'Buonarroti' Papworth designed a range of rustic fences, gates, and hurdles that can be easily and cheaply made. They can be constructed with unbarked coppiced wood, preferably hazel or ash, and members fastened together by thongs stripped from other branches. One only occasionally sees a rustic gate or fence, yet they are an attractive addition to a cottage or rustic garden (Plates 50 and 51).

Most people today have small gardens and if the decision is made to go rustic the unpretentious flowers of the cottage garden are the perfect choice. There is no better example than at Eastgrove Cottage Garden, north-west of Worcester. The garden is divided into different rooms by hedges and borders of old-fashioned favourites intermingled with more unusual plants. The colours are carefully coordinated. At the side of the house, deep coloured violas spill out from the trough below the pump, and are echoed more gently in the pale mauve of the wisteria that climbs the cottage walls. Beyond are spikes of dusty green-and-purple rosemary, and the whole picture is framed by an oak arch covered with pink roses. At the back of the house are the more vibrant colours, hot oranges, sharp yellows of verbascum, and more mellow golden rod. This is a garden for all seasons, but it is in the spring that the 'scree' garden, with its mounds of colour formed by the tiny alpines and saxifrages, is at its best. There are rustic benches which can be moved around to different positions as the garden changes through the year, and rustic arches that encapsulate pretty views of the garden and the countryside beyond. The rustic elements are unobtrusive, and blend perfectly with the multitude of colours and shapes in this 'olde worlde' garden.

10
RUSTIC GARDEN FURNITURE

The first record of furniture made from logs and branches is that of the bookcases designed by William Kent in 1735, for Merlin's Cave in the Royal Gardens at Richmond, to house the library of Stephen Duck (p. 48). Before this time, there appears to be no evidence of rustic furniture made from logs and branches. However, the fashion for rustic garden buildings in the eighteenth century brought with it a demand for rustic furniture, and from the mid-century some workshops and factories began to specialize in rustic items. On 13 July 1754 William Partridge, cabinet maker, advertised his 'Garden Seats, Windsor and Forest Chairs and Stools, in the modern, Gothic and Chinese taste . . .' in Jackson's *Oxford Journal*. The popularity of such furniture continued, and between 1790 and 1803, 'Stubbs's Manufactory' of City Road and Brick Lane, London, issued a trade card, advertising 'all sorts of Yew Tree, Gothic and Windsor Chairs, Alcoves and Rural Seats, Garden Machines, Dyed Chairs &c.'

Rustic furniture can be divided into three styles: first, the forest seats made from logs and branches; secondly, root furniture made from the roots of trees; and thirdly, the more sophisticated styles of rustic furniture found in the pattern books of cabinet makers from the 1760s onwards.

Forest seats and tables have enjoyed a long and continuing history, but there is no reference to this style of rustic furniture in early pattern books. The manufacture of forest furniture was, after all, a rural craft and it was probably unnecessary to provide patterns. Their construction uses basic joints, and relies on the individual's capacity for invention, and creative ability to use branches in the shapes that they present themselves.

Commonly built from felled trees or those damaged by storm, forest furniture was first made by country folk, or put together by the estate carpenter for the less formal walks of grand estates or to furnish the garden buildings. If constructed grotesquely enough, rustic furniture might have found a home in the hermitage. Solid and sturdy, yet cheap to make, forest furniture was sometimes used to contribute to the convivial atmosphere of the public pleasure garden of the city spas; forest seats are found outside many city public houses today. Forest furniture is suitable for almost any garden location, except perhaps the very formal walk, and even a simple bench, if carefully sited, can be an attractive addition to a garden.

There are no set rules as to whether bark should be left on the branches or stripped off. However, if branches are not stripped, the bark may peel off of its own account when left outside. Also, if bark is removed seasoning is hastened and strength increased. Nevertheless, good strong furniture can be made from green or 'wet' wood, as it is known in the trade. When peeled the surface revealed is often extremely beautiful and

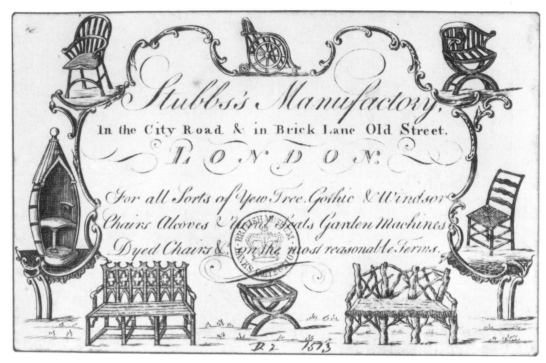

Trade card, 1790–1803

has a naturally polished surface. Stripping the bark also allows preservatives to penetrate the timber.

Bark stripping was once an important industry. The cut surface of alder trees and poles, stripped of their black bark in spring, reveals a bright-orange surface, betraying the usefulness of bark to the leather-tanning industry. These were both flourishing trades until the late nineteenth century, when bark-stripping finally became uneconomic.

Birch bark can be removed from trees in large plates. It is a waterproof material and was sometimes used by foresters for roofing temporary shelters. Lapps too, once used bark for roofing, and waterproof clothing was made by shaping pieces to protect body and limbs. It was particularly popular in Scandinavia, where it was used extensively in craftwork for plates, baskets, mats, alp-horns and bugles. Birch is perhaps the most beautiful of barks, and it has been widely used in the decoration of rustic features, sometimes applied as a veneer. The interior of the Bear's Hut, Killerton has a door veneered with bark. Victorian forest furniture was designed with and without the bark stripped, but in 1851, Shirley Hibberd, author of *Rustic Adornments for Homes of Taste*, turned his thoughts to the preservation of timber:

> Until the past ten years or so, manufacturers in the eastern parts of London made use of cheap oak timber, the produce for the most part of the pollard oaks of Epping Forest. This soon began to decay within by dry rot, which seldom gave any outward sign, so that a rustic structure in which the process had long been active, would preserve its respectable appearance until the final collapse came, when it would subside into a wreck, and, to the owner's surprise, be found to have long before consisted only of an outer shell of varnish or paint, and a mass of mere dust within.[1]

Although earlier craftsmen lacked modern knowledge of preservatives, they were concerned with preservation, and with prolonging the life of rustic properties.

Today, a coat of wood preservative under a coat of clear polyurethane is recommended. A flat finish is preferable to glossy, which tends to detract from the rustic appearance. Rustic furniture can also look very attractive if painted with flat green paint. If the furniture can be stored inside during the winter, so much the better. If left outside, it is a good idea to cover it with a waterproof sheet and to try to raise it off the ground by resting it on small pieces of paving.

In spite of some criticism the rustic style remained popular, and the third edition of Shirley Hibberd's *Rustic Adornments for Homes of Taste* continued to include illustrations of rustic sofas in the forest style. In 1840 T. J. Ricauti published his *Rustic Architecture*, which contained designs for a series of rustic dwellings but, alarmed by 'the obtrusive forms of crude and inelegant structures, whose outlines are anything but compatible with the surrounding scenery',[2] this was followed in 1842 by another handsomely produced volume, *Sketches for Rustic Work*. The book contains a number of drawings for garden baskets, chairs, and tables, and many designs use branches for the main structures and rods of wood in the twig mosaic style for decoration. The design of Ricauti's furniture is rather more formal than usual forest furniture. The covered seat has a Victorian primness about it and the accompanying chairs and bench too, are not made from rough-hewn and gnarled timber, but from cut poles. The geometric design indicates movement away from the grotesque, to a more ordered and pre-planned design, rather than creative innovation dictated by the shape of any timber to hand. As the century moved forward, writers continued to criticize forest furniture as badly made eyesores, but, nevertheless, in 1883, the famous gardener William Robinson suggested that 'old tree stumps help to make useful seats and the bole of the tree, if cut makes a very good seat.'[3] Today, around the Royal Park at Windsor, huge trunks from felled trees have been cut away to form comfortable settees. Nobody can deny they are an economical and attractive way of dealing with these huge timbers, as well as keeping them as part of the landscape. At Fanhams Hall, Hertfordshire, a roof has been built over an old tree stump to give shelter to a seat built around the remaining trunk. It is in an eye-catching position at the end of a tree-lined path.

By the 1900s the days of custom-built rustic furniture was fading fast, and seats, chairs, and tables of beautifully contorted shapes were becoming more and more scarce. One could pick up a catalogue and choose a standardized piece of rustic furniture, well designed and well made, but constructed with mainly straight poles, with perhaps a few gnarled and knotty pieces of branch for decoration. More frequently such furniture would be decorated with a simple lattice-work of straight branches. William Cooper Limited of the Old Kent Road, London, were well known for their rustic furniture, and a suite of two seats and a table, almost the same as the one shown on page 112, was available for the grand total of £2.7s.6d.; a rustic tree-seat, formed around the base of a tree trunk and described in their catalogue as 'useful for parties' could be supplied at 5s per foot run, with a footboard to match at 1s. per foot (and the finished seat was stained and varnished). Even at these prices, which now seem extraordinarily cheap, some people were still keen to try their own hand; Victorian magazines included articles on the subject, and by 1907 Paul Hasluck had compiled *Rustic Carpentry*, entirely devoted to rustic work.

Nineteenth-century forest furniture

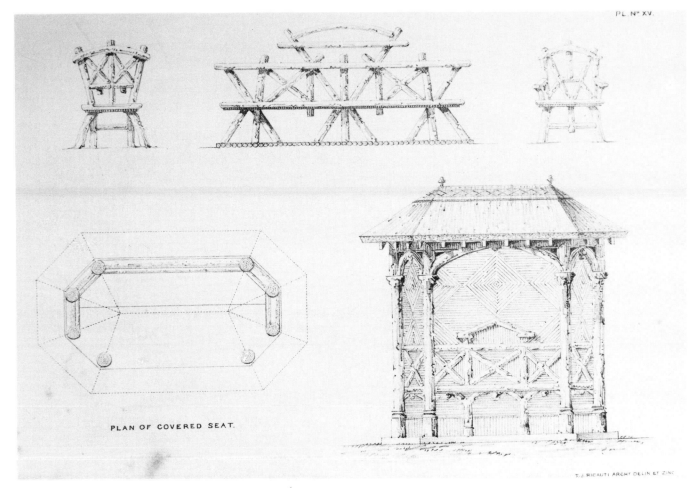

Covered seat and forest furniture, T. J. Ricauti, London, 1842

For Australian settlers rustic furniture was an essential. It was simply and cleverly styled from hand-adzed slabs, or shaped branches of eucalypt from the virgin forests. This furniture was strong and made to last. Now ranking among the nostalgic memorabilia of Australian bush heritage, these pieces are sought after as antiques.

Root furniture almost certainly originated in China, perhaps brought over to England by sailors or traders of the seventeenth and eighteenth century, and then copied by designers searching for novel ways of breaking with the classical idiom. In adopting this style they allowed themselves freedom to experiment using natural and exotic forms, which seemed to be part of nature herself, and satisfied their Romantic spirit. The method of construction is thought to be an old Chinese craft, and may have been practised by peasant communities. As an agricultural society the Chinese have learned to live frugally, and to use all available materials usefully and artistically. Some parts of China have few trees, and when used for timber even the roots cannot be ignored. There is still furniture of this style in garden pavilions in China, where it is proudly described as antique and examples can also be found in Chinese paintings and on porcelain of the Ch'ing Dynasty.

Root furniture is made by the contorting and carving of tree roots, which are welded together into intricate and densely woven forms that remain free-flowing so as to appear as if moulded into the shape required. If roots do not bend easily into shape they can be made more pliable by using steam. The Chinese also use this method for making plant baskets and pot stands. Grotesque in appearance, these pieces obviously played their part in contributing to the atmosphere of caprice and fantasy of Chinese garden pavilions, and frequently found a home in European grottoes and ornamental hermitages.

The earliest published designs of garden furniture were by Matthew Darly, in *A New Book of Chinese Designs* (1754). This book was mainly of oriental designs for japanners and painters, but designs for four root-chairs and a table were included. The chairs appear to be growing out of the ground itself, and each piece of furniture is apparently constructed from one piece of wood. The designs of Charles Over in his style book *Ornamental Architecture in the Gothic, Chinese and Modern Taste* (1758) have a direct link with this kind of design, and he stated that his rusticated arch was 'much used by the Chinese'.

The root furniture associated with the peasant crafts of China is not, as might be expected, roughly made. The proportions of the furniture in the Chinese pavilion illustrated are elegant, and the highly polished surfaces, perhaps achieved by using a clear lacquer, are fit for the grandest visitor (Plate 52). A quaint chair of Dr Nigel Temple is similar, but has a more open design and was probably formed from twisted pieces of willow and vine as well as root; it would certainly be at home in a hermitage.

The British painter Graham Sutherland (1903–1980), became well known for his semi-abstract scenes of desolation after bombing, painted when he was appointed official war artist in 1941. However, he was primarily interested in landscape, and fascinated by organic form. Sutherland made his first visit to the South of France in 1947, and later bought 'La Villa Blanche' at Menton. The main garden included an old olive grove and '...over the paths nearest the house were pergolas, fragrant with jasmin and roses; mimosa and hibiscus bloomed; and red and white datura...'[4] He became preoccupied with Mediterranean motifs and among his works is a series of paintings (1947–48) depicting vine pergolas; he was obviously fascinated by their contorted shapes. Sutherland also collected bits of trees and plants and began to paint a series of 'Standing Forms' developed from these pieces. When a new extension was added to the villa

> It was dominated by a handsome sitting room some 40 foot long with port-hole sky-lights echoing those in the original house. The floor was of honey-coloured Travertine marble, and the left-hand wall (largely sliding glass doors) gave onto a balcony overlooking the garden. The slightly austere effect was softened by a scattering of rugs, white sofas and arm chairs, some curious chairs made of twisted vine branches.[5]

A photograph also shows a large table made in the same style, not unlike the chair of Dr Temple, and it has been suggested that the furniture was made of gnarled olive branches, vine or roots. Many people find rustic furniture fascinating, and making it does present a challenge to those people with a creative spirit. Could it be, as some have suggested, that this furniture was made by Sutherland himself?

There were many designs for more sophisticated rustic garden furniture for

Root and vine chair belonging to Dr Nigel Temple

Rural Chairs   *for*   *Summer Houses*

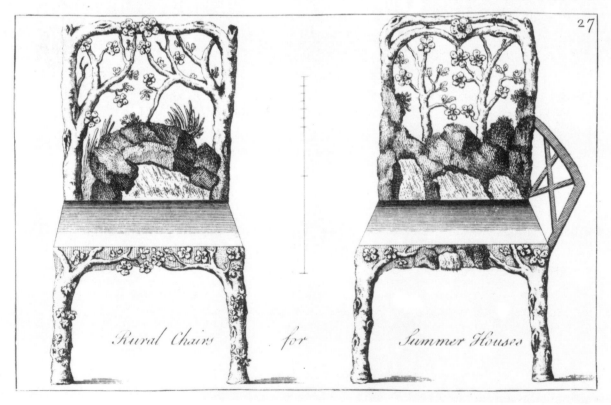

Rural Chairs   *for*   *Summer Houses*

Beech conservatory chairs, c.1770, believed to have originally come from Bagatelle

conservatory and garden rooms, but only a few of these designs were manufactured from rough-hewn timber. One designer in particular cannot be passed by: in 1765 Robert Manwaring published *The Cabinet and Chairmakers Real Friend and Companion*, in which 25 per cent of the plates are for 'Rural Chairs for Summerhouses and Rural Garden Seats'. Most of these designs are rustic and some are decorated with landscape paintings.

> The Designs given for rural Chairs for Summerhouses, Gardens, and Parks are entirely new, and are the only ones that ever were published ... I hope they will give general Satisfaction with respect to their Grandeur, Variety, Novelty and Usefulness; and if I succeed in this Point, I shall think myself amply satisfied for the Time and Trouble I have been at in composing them.[6]

Fourteen garden seats are illustrated, and five of them are in styles similar to those illustrated here. These are plainer in design than some of the other chairs in the book, and have flat wooden seats and aprons, but Manwaring instructs that the limbs are formed from rude branches of yew or apple trees, 'as nature produces them'.[7] He also recommends the

> ... stuff should be very dry and well-seasoned; after the bark is peeled clean off shute for your Pitches the nearest pieces you can match for the Shape of the Back, Fore Feet and Elbows.[8]

(Opposite:) Rural chairs for summerhouses, Robert Manwaring, 1765

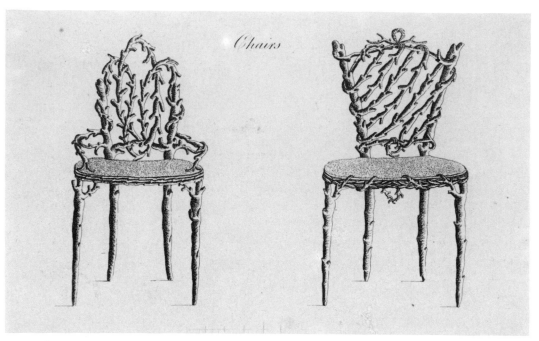

Rustic chairs, c.1797

The second pair of 'Rural Chairs' is based upon the same principles of construction, but is more ornate than the first pair. The prunus blossom is prolific, and the base of the chair back is painted, and sprouting clumps of carved grass. Manwaring suggests that 'the ornament may be painted green and will look very genteel'.[9]

A tradition of imitation rustic work developed, and in 1752 Matthias Lock and H. Copland published *A New Book of Ornaments*. This was the first book to contain rustic elements in the design of pieces of furniture for interiors. Some designers designed specifically for the carvers' trade. Small trees were carved into designs for household furniture, and frequently gilded. Some very fine pieces in the rustic style were used to furnish the grand houses of eighteenth-century Europe.[10] The Victoria and Albert Museum, London, holds a set of six chairs which closely resemble the style of Robert Manwaring. They are constructed in beechwood, carved in relief, and covered in gesso which is painted brown to simulate bark-covered branches, the smaller ones of which are lopped. The uprights and top rail are composed of continuous gnarled branches bound together at the centre of the top and lower rail. The back is filled with an open design of intertwining branches and all other members are in the same rusticated style. The seats are upholstered in brown leather. These chairs are believed to be *c.*1770 and it has been claimed that they came from the orangery of The Tuilleries Palace, and previously from Bagatelle.[11]

So popular was the rustic style in Great Britain, that it soon spread to France and Germany, where the enthusiasm of the publishers caused pirating of designs from English pattern books. (The preface to Manwaring's book suggests that he was aware of this.) From 1776 to 1887, the Parisienne publisher George Louis le Rouge issued 21 *cahiers* in the series *Detail de nouveaux jardins à la mode Jardins Anglo-Chinois*. 'Cahier LV' copied, in a reversed format and without acknowledgement, almost the whole of

A stool of mosaic twig-work standing on a floor of deers' knuckle-bones in the hermitage at Bicton Park, Devon

the illustrations of William Wrighte's *Grotesque Architecture; or, Rural Amusement of* 1767. The pirating of rustic furniture designs was also evident. Plates from *Rustic Furniture*, an undated and anonymous book printed for I. & J. Taylor, appeared in *Ideenmagazin für Liebhaber von Garten, Englischen Anlagen und für Besitzer von Landgütern* (Lepzig, 1797). However, the original remained a popular book, and was sold by I. & J. Taylor until at least 1838.

A chaise longue cast in concrete, Oakworth, Keighley, Lancashire

From the 1850s, in the Adirondack Mountains of the USA the fashion for rustic furniture moved from garden to house, but here, unlike the stately homes of Europe, the houses were log cabins and large timber buildings known as camps. The furniture was in a more country style, and much of it was as comfortable in the garden and on the porch as in the house, unlike the refined style of the grand European houses.

Stick furniture (which in England would be called forest furniture) was built from saplings or branches, often of birch, of about two inches in diameter, that were tied, wedged, or nailed together. Peeled poles and branches were used for more beautiful pieces, usually for indoor use, and boles of trees were frequently upturned, polished, and stood on a pedestal of roots to form tables. The Victorian practice of mosaic twig-work was adapted for the decoration of American country-style furniture: sideboards, chests, tables and sofas. Applied bark was also a speciality. Rustic-work remained popular through many decades in America, but between the 1930s and the early 1970s there was little demand. However, factory-produced rustic furniture is now available from department stores, or by mail order, and choice rustic pieces by contemporary craftsmen (rather than old-time rustic-workers) are available at Bloomingdales in New York.

The rustic idiom has been translated into a variety of materials, and the most well known is the much prized Victorian cast-iron furniture, now slavishly copied in pressed steel. Less well known are the concrete benches at Oakworth House, Keighley. At Keighley, a rockery and conservatory were designed by the Frenchman Aucaunte, in the second half of the nineteenth century, following the fashion set in the Parisian parks. Outside in the grounds he built a summerhouse, and concrete benches shaped as if from natural unbarked branches.[12]

Glazed stoneware chair

Glazed stoneware chair

Last but not least are the rustic-style glazed stoneware garden furniture and urns, manufactured by the Hurlford Fire Clay Works, Kilmarnock, in the mid-nineteenth century. These pieces are seldom seen today, and when they are they command very high prices in the saleroom. The furniture is glazed brown in colour or perhaps brown and green. The chairs usually stand over 40 inches high, are solid, sturdy, and have the appearance of heavy tree stumps. Branches growing from the stumps sprout oak leaves to form grotesque, amorphous branch arms and backs.

The modern materials chosen to imitate rustic-work of logs and branches are all more durable nowadays, but nonetheless fanciful. I have yet to come across rustic designs in plastic, but who knows what the future might bring!

NOTES

1 Castle and Farm

1 MOUNTAINE, DIDYMUS, *The Gardener's Labyrinth*, London, 1577. Quoted in Blomfield, R., *The Formal Garden in England*, 3rd edition, Macmillan, 1901.

2 HALL, Sir JAMES. 'The Origin and Principles of Gothic Architecture', *The Transactions of the Royal Academy of Edinburgh*, 6 April 1797.

3 Ibid.

4 CARSE, ALEXANDER, came from Edinburgh and is best known for his genre paintings, e.g. 'The Penny Wedding' (1819), now in the National Gallery of Scotland. 'The Willow Cathedral' is thought to be his earliest work.

5 HALL, op.cit.

2 The Natural Style

1 The Grand Tour was the journey made to Italy by wealthy eighteenth-century Englishmen in order to complete their education by absorbing classical culture. The most tangible result was usually the acquisition of a collection of old masters and antique sculptures.

2 CHAMBERS, Sir WILLIAM, *Designs of Chinese Buildings, Furniture, Dresses, Machines and Utensils*, 1757.

3 CHAMBERS, Sir WILLIAM, *A Treatise on the Decorative Part of Civil Architecture*, 1759.

4 WRIGHT, THOMAS, *Universal Architecture, Six Original Designs of Arbours*, 1755 (ed. EILEEN HARRIS, Scolar Press, 1979). A facsimile of the two parts of *Universal Architecture* (1755 and 1758) with a catalogue of Wright's works in architecture and garden design.

5 ALLAN, GEORGE, 'A sketch of the character of Mr. Thomas Wright', *Gentleman's Magazine*, 1793.

6 HARRIS, op. cit.

7 WRIGHT, THOMAS, op. cit.

8 DUNZHEN, LIU, 'The Traditional Gardens of Suzhou' (trs. Frances Wood), *Garden History, The Journal of the Garden History Society*, vol. 10, no. 2, Autumn 1982.

9 LAMBERT, D. and HARDING, S., 'Thomas Wright at Stoke Park', *Garden History, The Journal of the Garden History Society*, vol. 17, no. 1, Spring 1989.

10 Ex. inf. the permanent exhibition at The Jenner Museum, Berkeley. I am indebted to Ms D. Rawlinson of The Jenner Museum for her help.

11 OVER, CHARLES, *Ornamental Architecture in the Gothic, Chinese and Modern Taste*, 1758.

12 The Devonshire Collections: the 6th Duke's Handbook, 1844. Ex. inf. Peter Day, Keeper of Collections, Chatsworth.

13 The Devonshire Collections: eighteenth-century accounts. Ex. inf. Peter Day, Keeper of Collections, Chatsworth.

3 Hermits and Hermitages

1 PRATT, E. A., *A History of Inland Transport and Communication*, (new ed. 1970). Quoted in HIBBERT, C., *The English*, Guild, 1987.

2 CHAMBERS, Sir WILLIAM, *Designs of Chinese Buildings, Furniture, Dresses, Machines and Utensils*, 1757.

3 SENG-YU (poet, sixth-century AD), in KING, R., *Great Gardens of the World*, Peerage, 1979.

4 WRIGHTE, WILLIAM, *Grotesque Architecture; or, Rural Amusement*, 1767.

5 OVER, CHARLES, *Ornamental Architecture in the Gothic, Chinese and Modern Taste*, Sayer, 1758.

6 ROTH, WARWICK, *Pleasure Gardens of the Eighteenth Century*, Macmillan, 1896.

7 KNIGHT, ALMON, *An Heroic Epistle to Sir William Chambers*, 1772 (6th edition).

8 According to the Badminton Estate Papers, from 1746 Kent was still involved in putting up battlements at Holly Bush House, Badminton. Thomas Wright had completed the ' "hermit house" or "hermitage" including felling trees for the hermitage' by October 1747. Margaret Richards suggests that it is, therefore, possible that William Kent and Thomas Wright worked contemporaneously at Badminton. Gloucester Records Office, ref. QB3/3/1.

9 WRIGHT, THOMAS, *Universal Architecture*, 1755.

10 JONES, BARBARA, *Follies and Grottoes*, Constable, 1979.

11 Miscellaneous verses, memoranda etc., including 'motto's in the Cell: over the entrance' and 'on the ground...' (*c.* 1747). Badminton Muniment Fmk, 1/4/4.

12 Ibid.

13 Ibid.

14 FESTING, S., 'Notes and Queries: Amateur and Professional Hermits', *Garden History Society: Newsletter 14*, Summer 1985 and *Newsletter 15*, Autumn, 1985.

15 TIMBS, JOHN, *English Eccentrics*, 1866.

16 Ibid.

17 Ibid.

18 SITWELL, E., *English Eccentrics*, Penguin, 1958.

19 HUSSEY, CHRISTOPHER, *The Picturesque*, Putnam, 1927.

20 TIMBS, op. cit.

21 STURMAN, CHRISTOPHER, 'A Lincolnshire Hermit: Wolley Jolland (1745–1831)', *Report and Journal of the Georgian Society*, 1987. I am indebted to Mr Sturman for much information.

22 REPTON, HUMPHRY, 'Memoirs' (compiled 1814). Printed in CARTER, G., GOODE, P. and LAURIE, K., *Humphry Repton, Landscape Gardener 1752–1818*, 1983, and STURMAN, op. cit.

23 Ibid.

24 STURMAN, C., op. cit.

25 Ibid.

26 Ibid.

27 Ibid., 'Lincoln, Rutland and Stamford Mercury', 19 August 1831.

28 Ibid., advertisement of sale.

29 REPTON, HUMPHRY, 'Memoirs' (compiled 1814) in STURMAN, C., op. cit.

4 The Picturesque and its Legacy

1 JELLICO, G. and S., GOODE, P., and LANCASTER, M., *The Oxford Companion to Gardens*, Oxford University Press, 1986.
2 GILPIN, WILLIAM, 'Observations, Relative Chiefly to Picturesque Beauty made in the year 1772, on several parts of England; particularly the Mountains and Lakes of Cumberland, and Westmoreland', Blamire, 1886.
3 TEMPLE, NIGEL, *John Nash and the Village Picturesque*, Sutton, 1979.
4 LOUDON, J. C. (ed.) *The Landscape Gardening and Landscape Architecture of the late Humphry Repton, Esq.*, 1840.
5 TEMPLE, op. cit.
6 MURRAY'S *Hertfordshire, Bedfordshire and Buckinghamshire*, 1895.
7 PAPWORTH, WYATT A., *John B. Papworth, Architect to The King of Wurtemburg. A Brief Record of His Life and Works; being a contribution to the History of Art and Architecture during the period 1775–1847.*
8 HOFLAND, B., *A Description of the Mansion of Whiteknights*, 1819.
9 Ibid.
10 Ibid.
11 Ibid.
12 JELLICOE et al., op. cit.
13 DOWNING, ANDREW JACKSON, *Cottage Residences*, Wiley and Putnam, 1842.
14 'Gardenesque': a term coined by J. C. Loudon in 1832 to describe a style of planting design in which each individual plant is allowed to develop its natural character as fully as possible in garden conditions. However, it came to be used to describe the mixed style of garden design favoured by the Victorians, e.g. as found at Alton Towers and Biddulph Grange.

5 The Victorian Rustic Garden

1 The card was designed by John Calcot Horseley at the suggestion of Henry Cole, who went on to found what is now the Victoria and Albert Museum. Almost 1000 copies were lithographed and coloured by hand to be sold at one shilling each.
2 ACLAND, A., *Killerton*, The National Trust, 1986.
3 Ibid.
4 BLAKELEE, G. E., *The Home Workshop*, Simpkin, Marshall, Hamilton, Kent & Co. (publication date not given).
5 Ibid.
6 Ibid.

6 New Technology

1 HITCHCOCK, H. R., *The Pelican History of Art. Architecture: Nineteenth and Twentieth Centuries*, Penguin, 1977.
2 ROBINSON, W., *The Parks, Promenades, and Gardens of Paris*, 1869.
3 Ex inf. Jacques Gerard, Parc Botanique de la Fosse.
4 ELLIOTT, B., *Victorian Gardens*, Batsford, 1986.

7 The Edwardian Rustic Garden

1 PLUMPTRE, G., *Collins Book of British Gardens*, 1985.

2 Ex inf. National Trust permanent exhibition, Clandon Park.
3 WAUGH, A., *The Lipton Story*, Cassell, 1951.
4 VASARI, G. (1568) (trans. de VERE 1912–15) *The Lives of the Artists*, Warner, 1976.
5 FORSYTH, A., *Yesterday's Gardens*, HMSO, 1983.
6 RABINOWITZ, J., 'Place for Relaxation, Site of Eternal Beauty', *Ikebana International*, no. 46, 1976.
7 LOWENTHAL, H., et al., *The Edward James Foundation*, (ed. NOEL SIMON), 1981.

8 Royalty, Writers and the Rustic Taste

1 DUNLOP, I., *The Country around Paris*, Collins, 1986.
2 Ibid.
3 PLUMPTRE, G., *Royal Gardens*, Collins, 1981.
4 BOSWELL, J., *The Life of Johnson* (L. F. Powell's revision of G. G. Hills ed.) (written in 1777).
5 The summerhouse was unfortunately destroyed by fire in May 1991.
6 WORDSWORTH, D., *Journal of Dorothy Wordsworth*, (ed. MOORMAN, M.) 1971.
7 Ibid.
8 WATTS, A. S., *Dickens at Gad's Hill*, Elvenden Press, 1989.

10 Rustic Garden Furniture

1 HIBBERD, SHIRLEY, *Rustic Adornments for Homes of Taste*, Groombridge, 1870.
2 RICAUTI, T. J., *Sketches for Rusticwork*, 1842.
3 ROBINSON, WILLIAM, *The English Flower Garden and Home Ground*, Murray, 1900.
4 BERTHOUD, ROGER, *Graham Sutherland*, A Biography, Faber, 1982.
5 Ibid.
6 MANWARING, ROBERT, *The Cabinet and Chairmaker's Real Friend and Companion*, 1765.
7 Ibid.
8 MANWARING, op. cit.
9 MANWARING, op. cit.
10 A very fine console table with naturalistic tree trunks by the eighteenth-century designer and carver Thomas Johnson was offered at auction by Christie's in 1986 and carved pieces are to be found in the Palace of Het Loo, Holland.
11 Ex. inf. Victoria and Albert Museum. Register No. W.61 to 66 – 1952. A set of these chairs have now been copied and can be seen at The Swiss Cottage, Cahir, Co. Tipperary, Eire.
12 ELLIOTT, BRENT, *Victorian Gardens*, Batsford, 1986.

BIBLIOGRAPHY

ACLAND, A., 1986: *Killerton*

ALPHAND, A., 1876: *Les Promenades de Paris*

ANDRÉ, E., 1879: *Parcs et Jardins*

ANON, 1838: *Ideas for Rustic Furniture*

ARNOLD, J., 1975: *All Made by Hand*

BERTHOUD, R., 1982: *Graham Sutherland, A Biography*

BLAKELEE, G. E., c.1850: *The Home Workshop*

BLOMFIELD, R., 1901: *The formal Garden in England*

BRANZI, A., 1985: *Domestic Animals*

CARTER *et al.*, 1983 (George Carter, Patrick Goode and Kedrun Laurie): *Humphry Repton, Landscape Designer, 1752–1818*

CHAMBERS, W., 1757: *Designs of Chinese Buildings, Furniture, Dresses, Machines and Utensils*

CHAMBERS, W., 1759: *A Treatise on the Decorative Part of Civil Architecture*

CHAMBERS, W., 1772: *A Dissertation on Oriental Gardening*

CLIFTON-TAYLOR, A., 1980: *The Pattern of English Building*

CONNER, P., 1979: *Oriental Architecture in the West*

COOK, R., 1974: *The Tree of Life*

COX, P. and STACEY, W., 1972: *The Australian Homestead*

DARLEY, G., 1975: *Villages of Vision*

DARLEY, G., 1976: *The Idea of the Village*

DARLY, M., 1766: *The Chairmaker's Guide*

DOWNING, A. J., 1842: *Cottage Residences*

DOWNING, A. J., 1849: *A Treatise on the Theory and Practice of Landscape Gardening, Adapted to North America*

DOWNING, A. J., 1853: *Rural Essays*

DRESSER, C., 1882: *Japan, Its Architecture, Art and Art Manufacturers*

DUNLOP, I., 1986: *The Country Around Paris*

DUNZHEN, L., 1986 (trans. Frances Wood): 'The traditional Gardens of Suzhou', *Garden History: Journal of the Garden History Society*

EDLIN, H. L., 1949: *Woodland Crafts in Britain*

EDWARDS, P., 1965: *English Garden Ornament*

ELLIOTT, B., 1987: *Victorian Gardens*

FESTING, S., 1985: 'Amateur and Professional Hermits', *The Garden History Society: News Letter 14*

FLORANCE, A., 1987: *Queen Victoria at Osborne*

FORSYTH, A., 1983: *Yesterday's Gardens*

GILBORN, C., 1987: *Adirondack Furniture and the Rustic Tradition*

GILPIN, W., 1782: *Observations on the River Wye, and Several Parts of South Wales, &c. Relative Chiefly to Picturesque Beauty; Made in the Summer of the Year 1770*

GILPIN, W., 1786: *Observations, Relative Chiefly to Picturesque Beauty, made in the year 1772, on several parts of England; Particularly the Mountains, and Lakes of Cumberland, and Westmorland*

GLOAG, J. E., 1964: *The Englishman's Chair*

GLOAG, J. E., 1970: *Mr Loudon's England*

GOTHEIN, M. L., 1928: *A History of Garden Art, Vols 1 and 2*

GROHMANN, J., 1797: *Ideenmagazin für Lieberhaber von Garten, Englischen Anlagen und für Besitzer von Landgütern*

HALL, Sir J., 1797: 'Essay on the Origin and Principles of Gothic Architecture', *Transactions of the Royal Academy of Edinburgh*

HALL, Sir J., 1813: *Essay on the Origin and Principles of Gothic Architecture* (with many illustrations, believed to be by Blore)

HARVEY, J., 1988: *Restoring Period Gardens*

HASLUK, P., 1907: *Rustic Furniture*

HECKSCHER, M., 1975: 'Eighteenth Century Rustic Furniture Designs', *The Journal of The Furniture History Society*, Vol. X1

HENSLOW, T. G. W., 1924: *Garden Improvement*

HERMAN, W., 1962: *Laugier and the 18c French Theory*

HIBBERT, C., 1987: *The English: A Social History 1066–1945*

HIBBERD, S., 1870 (3rd ed.): *Rustic Adornments for Homes of Taste*

HIBBERD, S., 1878: *The Amateur's Flower Garden*

HITCHCOCK, H. R., 1977: *The Pelican History of Art: Architecture: Nineteenth and Twentieth Centuries*

HOFLAND, B., 1819: *A Descriptive Account of the Mansion and Gardens of Whiteknights, Seat of the Duke of Marlborough*

HOOPER, T., 1985: *The Illustrated Encyclopedia of Beekeeping*

HUMPHREYS, P.W., 1914: *Garden Architecture*

HUNT, J. D., 1987: *William Kent, Landscape Garden Designer: An Assessment and Catalogue of His Designs*

HUNT, P., 1974: *The Book of Garden Ornament*

HUSSEY, C., 1927: *The Picturesque, Studies in a Point of View*

HYDE, M., 1973: *The Impossible Friendship*

INGPEN, R., 1927: *Pioneer Settlement in Australia*

JACQUES, D., 1983: *Georgian Gardens; The Reign of Nature*

JONES, B., 1979: *Follies and Grottoes*

LAMBERT, D. and HARDING, S., 1989: 'Thomas Wright at Stoke Park', *Garden History: The Journal of the Garden History Society*

LOUDON, J. C., 1836: *Encyclopedia of Cottage, Farm and Villa Architecture*

LOUDON, J. C., 1840: *The Landscape Gardening of the late Humphrey Repton*

LOUDON, J., 1840: *Practical Instruction in Gardening for Ladies*

LOUDON, J., 1841: *The Ladies' Companion to the Flower Garden*

LOUDON, J., 1848 (ed. Downing, A. J.): *Gardening for Ladies; and Companion to The Flower Garden*

LOWENTHAL, H. *et al.*, 1981: *The Edward James Foundation*

MANWARING, R. (ed. Simon, N.) 1765: *The Cabinet and Chairmaker's Real Friend and Companion*

M'INTOSH, C., 1938: *The Flower Garden*

MOORMAN, M., 1965: *William Wordsworth, The Later Years, 1803–1850*

NICHOLS, B., 1926: *Twenty Five, A Young Man's Candid Recollections of His Elders and Betters*

OVER, C., 1758: *Ornamental Architecture in the Gothic, Chinese and Modern Taste*

PAPWORTH, W., 1879: *John P. Papworth, Architect to The King of Wurtemburg*

PAPWORTH, J. B., 1818: *Rural Residences*

PAPWORTH, J. B., 1823: *Hints on Ornamental Gardening*

PETIT, V., 1848: *Habitations champêtres*

PLUMPTRE, G., 1981: *Royal Gardens*

PRICE, U., 1796–98: *Essays on the Picturesque, as Compared with the Sublime and the Beautiful*

RABINOWITZ, J., 1976: 'Place for Relaxation, Site of Eternal Beauty', *Ikebana International No. 46*

REPTON, H., 1806: *Forming Country Residences, 1806*

REPTON, H., 1840 (ed. Loudon, J. C.): *The Landscape Gardening and Landscape Architecture of the Late Humphrey Repton, Esq.*

RICAUTI, T. J., 1840: *Rustic Architecture*

RICAUTI, T. J., 1842: *Sketches for Rustic Work*

ROBINSON, J. M., 1988: *The English Country Estate*

ROBINSON, W., 1868: *The Parks, Promenades, and Gardens of Paris*

ROBINSON, W., 1900: *The English Flower Garden and Home Ground*

RYKERT, J., 1972: *Adam's Hut in Paradise*

SIREN, O., 1950: *China and the Gardens of Europe of the 18c.*

SITWELL, Dame E., 1958: *English Eccentrics*

SMITH, E., 1957: *A History of Whiteknights*

STEPHENSON, S. H., 1979: *Rustic Furniture*

STURMAN, C., 1987: 'A Lincolnshire Hermit: Wolley Jolland (1745–1831), *The Report and Journal of the Georgian Society*

TEMPLE, Dr N., 1979: *John Nash and the Village Picturesque*

THOMAS, G. S., 1979: *Gardens of the National Trust*

TIMBS, J., 1866: *English Eccentrics and Eccentricities*

TURNER, R., 1989: *Jim Partridge: Woodworker*

VARDY, J., 1744: *Some Designs of Inigo Jones and William Kent*

VASARI, G., 1568 (trans. de Vere): *The Lives of the Artists*

VAUX, C., 1874: *Villas and Cottages*

WARD, C., 1912: *Royal Gardens*

WATTS, A., 1989: *Dickens at Gad's Hill*

WAUGH, A., 1951: *The Lipton Story*

WORDSWORTH, D., (ed. Moorman, M.), 1971: *The Journal of Dorothy Wordsworth*

WRIGHT, T., 1755 and 1758: *Universal Architecture, Arbours and Grottos.* (A facsimile of the two parts of *Universal Architecture*, with a catalogue of Wright's works in architecture and garden design by Eileen Harris, 1979.)

WRIGHTE, W., 1767: *Grotesque Architecture; or, Rural Amusement*

2

PLACES TO VISIT

The Adirondack Museum, Blue Mountain Lake, NY, 12812, USA (tel. 518-352-7311)
Bicton Park, East Budleigh, Budleigh Salterton, Devon EX9 7DP (tel. 0395 68465)
Biddulph Grange Garden, Biddulph, Stoke-on-Trent (tel. 074 377 649)
Parc Buttes Chaumont, Paris, France
Charles Dickens Centre, Eastgate House, High Street, Rochester, Kent (tel. 0634 43666)
Chatsworth, Bakewell, Derbyshire, DE4 1PP (tel. 024 688 2204)
Clandon Park, West Clandon, Guildford GU4 7RQ (tel. 0483 222482)
Cliveden, Maidenhead, Berkshire, SL6 0JA (tel. 0628 605069)
Eastgrove Cottage Garden Nursery, Sankyns Green, Little Witley, Worcester
    (tel. 0229 896389)
Parc Botanique de la Fosse, Fontaine-les Coteaux, Loir-et-Cher, 41800, Montoire, France
    (tel. 54 85 63)
Frogmore Gardens, Windsor, Berkshire. (Information: National Garden Scheme.)
    (tel. 071 730 0359)
Furzey Garden, Minstead, nr Lyndhurst, Hampshire (tel. 0703 812464)
Grizedale Forest Park, Grizedale, Cumbria (tel. 022 984 373)
Hawkstone Park, Weston-under-Redcastle, Shrewsbury, SY4 5UY (tel. 093924 611)
Heale House Gardens, Middle Woodford, nr Salisbury, Wiltshire, SP4 6NT
    (tel. 0722 73207)
Iford Manor Gardens, Bradford-on-Avon (tel. 022 16 3146)
Le Jardin des Plantes, Paris, France
The Jenner Museum, The Chantry, Church Lane, Berkeley, Gloucestershire
    (tel. 0453 810631)
Kenmore and Taymouth Castle, Perthshire, Scotland
Killerton, Broadclyst, Exeter, Devon EX5 3LE (tel. 0392 881 345)
Osborne House, Isle of Wight (tel. 0983 852484)
Polesden Lacey, nr Dorking, Surrey RH5 6BD (tel. 0372 58203)
Queen Eleanor's Garden, Great Hall, Winchester Castle, Hampshire
Rippon Lea, Melbourne, Australia (tel. 523 9150)
Rydal Mount, nr Ambleside, Cumbria (tel. 05394 33002)
Sandringham House and Grounds, Norfolk. (Enquiries: tel. 0553 772675)
Spetchley Park, Spetchley, nr Worcester (tel. 090 565 213/224)
The Swiss Garden, Old Warden, Bedfordshire (tel. 0234 56181)
Weald and Downland Open Air Museum, Singleton, Chichester, Sussex (tel. 0243 63 348)
West Dean Gardens, West Dean, Chichester, Sussex (tel. 024 363 303)
Woodland Park and Woodland Heritage Museum, Brokerswood, Westbury, Wiltshire, BA13
    4EH (tel. 0373 822238)

USEFUL ADDRESSES

Sun Designs publish a series of books containing drawings for garden buildings e.g. The Sprout House, Northenaire Privy, Alpine Swiss Cottage, and Yukon Bridge, shown in this book, and plans are available by post. Enquiries: Sun Designs, P.O. Box 206, Delafield, WI 53018. USA.

The National Society of Master Thatchers will give advice on thatching and recommend thatchers and builders of rustic garden buildings: Enquiries: Christopher White, 73 Hughenden Avenue, Downley, High Wycombe, Bucks, HP13 5SL.

Woven willow garden features from hurdles to summerhouses are available from the manufacturer: The English Basket Centre, The Willows, Curload, Stoke St. Gregory, nr Taunton, Somerset (tel. 0823 69418); and from the stockist: English Water Gardens, Rock Lane, Washington, West Sussex, RH20 3BL (tel. 903 892006).

Willow sculpture is made by: Madeline Gould, The Birches, Brake Lane, Hagley, Stourbridge, West Midlands, DY8 2XM.

INDEX